We Don't Push in Fairhope

Also by Leslie Anne Tarabella

The Majorettes Are Back in Town
Exploding Hushpuppies
Bringing Christmas Home

We Don't Push in Fairhope

Leslie Anne Tarabella

Liberty Blue Press

Copyright © 2024 by Leslie Anne Tarabella

All rights reserved. No part of this publication may be reproduced, distributed or transmitted in any form or by any means, including photocopying, recording, or other electronic or mechanical methods, without the prior written permission of the publisher, except in the case of brief quotations embodied in critical reviews and certain other non-commercial uses permitted by copyright law.

All brand names and trademarks mentioned in this book are the property of their respective owners. The mention of specific companies or products does not imply any affiliation with or endorsement by them.

Photos by Leslie Anne and Robert M. Tarabella.
Cover design by Jody Cory.

We Don't Push in Fairhope / Leslie Anne Tarabella
ISBN: 979-8-9883884-2-5

This book is dedicated
to all Fairhopers, past, present, and future, and
to those who have ever loved their own small town.

One place understood helps us understand all places better.
— Eudora Welty

Contents

Introduction 3
This Is My Story 5
Fairhopers or Fairhopians? 11
Hey, Don't Push! 15
How Did You Get Here? 29
Reverse Seinfeld 35
The Truth About Newcomers 39
Meanwhile, in the Coffee Shop 43
18 Rules 47
A Fair Hope of Success 51
Operation Home Sweet Home 55
The Clock 60
The Post Office 63
Served Up Right 69
For Everything There Is a Season 75
A Small Spiffy Southern Town 79
Don't Throw That Jar Away 89
An Afternoon at the Ballet 95
It's Just "Stuff" 99
Would You Live in an Agrihood? 103
Overheard in Latte Da 107
Hop on the Walking School Bus 109
Two New Activities 113
Santa Knows She Pushed 117
The Dog Days in Fairhope 123
Sign of the Times 127
Neighborhood Bridges 131

Meanwhile at the Nail Salon	137
Let's Give Them Something to Talk About	141
Food, Nutrition and Kindness	147
Infrastructure	151
Here's a Bit of Advice	157
The Pandemic	161
Alligators in the Bay	173
Barbecue is Not an Event	179
A Dream Come True	187
This Little Light of Mine	191
Why Thursdays?	195
Campers in Love	197
Talent Beyond Limits	205
928 Is Oh, So Great	211
Meanwhile At the Clubhouse	213
Good, Bad, and Ugly	217
The Surprise at the Museum	221
Twilight Wish	225
Could We Be Paris?	227
Dear Florala	231
Just Because You Can Doesn't Mean You Should	235
Before You Call the Moving Truck	239
Worthy of Praise	245
Goodbye to Fairhope	247
Acknowledgments	251
About the Author	253

We Don't Push in Fairhope

Introduction

Originally conceived as a utopian experiment, Fairhope, Alabama, has undergone a remarkable evolution over the years. From its roots as an economic experiment, it has transformed into an artist's colony and intellectual retreat and is today recognized as a boutique resort town.

Founded in 1894 as a Single Tax colony based on the philosophy of economist Henry George, the small town on Mobile Bay attracted scholars and dreamers. In 1907, Marietta Johnson founded the School for Organic Education, a pioneering institution that John Dewey included in his 1915 book, Schools of Tomorrow.

The uniqueness of Fairhope is even found in nature when a Jubilee occurs, causing marine life to swim ashore in the pre-dawn hours, which allows early-rising residents to partake in an easy seafood catch. This phenomenon is only documented in two places in the entire world.

The following stories are true with the names of real people included when possible unless they are changed to protect their personal feelings, job or reputation. In that case, the story may be embellished or jiggled around to hide their identity or stretched to make them sound far more interesting than they actually are which is sometimes required by law for Southern storytelling, especially if it involves a fish. Fairhope, Alabama, however, is a very real place, just like heaven.

1
This Is My Story

Have Americans suddenly realized sweet tea is the fountain of youth? Are they dreaming of dirt roads and craving grits? No matter what their true reason may be, everyone seems to be reenacting the Jed Clampett story, loading up their trucks and moving to L.A. – Lower Alabama.

This collection of stories isn't a declaration that Fairhope, Alabama, is better than any other city. Instead, it serves as a reflection of the home where I've lived since 1999. It also isn't a scientific analysis of why or how it has become so popular. Instead, it's a fun look at our much-publicized town's local flavor, quirks, and unique personalities.

In between the stories of people, places and traditions, you'll come to see why seemingly every newspaper, magazine, and social media maven wants to publicize our small town by awarding it the honor of "best of" something or the other. Fairhope has earned the titles of "best small town," "best place to retire," "best place to see a bird fly," "best place to slurp a real oyster," "best place to get your roots touched up," "best place to have Barbie and Ken as your neighbor," "best place to find God," "best place to lose your religion," "best place to raise children," "best place to ruin your children," and let's not forget the most magnificent honor, "best place to be buried next to a trailer park just off the four-lane."

My husband and I moved to Fairhope not only for the benefits of small-town life, but also to be close to my Gulf Coast family without living in the same town. I'm sure many of you understand that particular family plan — close but not too close.

We thought we'd live and die in a small town, but like other similarly sized cities in this region, Fairhope has grown like kudzu in a heat wave, doubled in size, and has seen home prices skyrocket. Although schools, roads, and restaurants have become overcrowded, more people continue to move here. Even when we travel to faraway places, it seems everyone there already knows about Fairhope and claps their hands together as they tell us how they "love-love-love it!" There's a mystique about some places that can't be explained, and our hometown is one of them.

This Is My Story

There are already plenty of history books about Fairhope, so I won't attempt to duplicate those. There's also a mound of articles with glowing chamber of commerce–style stories. Unfortunately, many of these have been written by people who have only stopped long enough to grab a bowl of gumbo, or vacationed here once as a child. The author's memories of eating a bologna sandwich while dangling their legs off a pier are sweet, but they now feel qualified to write about our town as if they were born beneath a magnolia tree at the foot of the Orange Street Pier during a moonlit Jubilee, then adopted and raised by Marietta Johnson herself.

I'll stick to what I know, and that's what Fairhope means to me and what it has been like to live here for over a quarter of a century. Everything is changing so fast; it's hard to describe, yet in my research, people in the 1920s, then again in the 1970s, felt the same edginess of change.

Sometimes I think our city motto should be, "Who are all these people?"

The stories in this book are a current-day snapshot of the home where I've lived, loved, laughed, cried, cursed, voted, danced, parented, shopped, boycotted, celebrated, mourned, and will someday die. I was born in South Alabama, and thanks to Google Maps, I know that I spent my childhood only 42.7 miles from where I live today.

Living here not nearly as long as some, yet these days, longer and longer than most, I've grown into a real Fairhoper. As I've become entwined in the community, this small town has both bruised and nourished my heart, making it a true home. It has been a delicate, sweet-and-sour marinade of life, and I'm a better person for it.

Here's the spoiler alert: The uniting theme of this collection of stories isn't flowers or sunsets. It's connections. Searching for connections is what draws people to a place, not the pretty bijou beads, bobbles, and bows. How do you find, grow, and keep connectivity? Through these tales of people and places, you'll see how the citizens of Fairhope use connections to create a charming and desirable place to live.

The intense anger and violence seen across America in recent years has, for the most part, been avoided in our small town. Although the citizens of Fairhope are opinionated, they still have Southern manners that prevent them from leaping into giant slug-fests. Everyone knows that only petite slug-o-ramas are permitted and must be followed by a sincere note of apology.

I've consciously decided to avoid current hot-button issues by wearing my prescription-mandated rose-colored glasses. There's no need to jump on the bandwagon of angry finger-wagging and shouting when we're all sick and tired of negativity, and besides, there are so many other wonderful things to celebrate; it's good to focus on those. And like the friend who wiped out on the dance floor at the Mardi Gras Ball and ended up in Thomas Hospital with a severely sprained "boom-boom" and a torn

This Is My Story

"hitchy-ma-call-it," we hope the painful moments are soon forgotten, and only the sparkly loveliness is remembered.

If you put 300 Fairhope residents in a room and asked them to describe this place, you'd get 300 different responses. My description is: Fairhope's not perfect, but it's the home I love.

You may agree or disagree.

Just don't push us around.

Whenever a kid loses a tooth, Fairhope throws a parade.
— **William Stitt**, owner of Bill-E's Restaurant and Bill-E's Small Batch Bacon

2

Fairhopers or Fairhopians?

"Fairhopers" or "Fairhopians"? It's a debate that will split the Lovely Ladies' Lunch Club slap down the middle. "My great-granddaddy said we were 'Fairhopers!'" insisted Reeva Rae. "Humph!" snorted Mary Nell. "'Fairhopians' has a ring that sounds like the bells in heaven, and you know it."

This same conversation occurs in one form or another several times a day somewhere in Fairhope.

Like most Southerners, we can complicate the tiniest things and make majestic mountains out of molehills. We can elevate a simple school issue into a war or spend millions of dollars arguing over a tiny sliver of land. We regularly pat our politicians on the back then plan to run them out of town later that week, so to disagree about what we're called is no big deal. "Sometimes, the debate is more fun than the solution," mused George while waiting on his pecan-pimento cheese order in Greer's Deli.

But what keeps us sane and eludes controversy are two simple principles; life here is good, and we know it.

When the day begins, we pass people walking, running, and driving down the streets. They give the nod, or wave, which is an automatic custom, and we know this simple gesture doesn't just mean, "Hey, there." It really means, "I'm glad you're my neighbor."

Our flower-topped garbage cans and light posts spill colorful joy onto the streets as the city workers maintain the behind the scenes greenhouses that burst with seasonal blooms.

We run into people like our expert local historian, Donnie Barrett, who told me, "Yes, I prefer Fairhopers because the early settlers called themselves that in the 1920s after they realized how their experimental town was going to work, but not before."

With approval from Donnie, we can confidently say Fairhopers go to work in small offices, downtown shops, art galleries, home offices, or even coffee shops where they work remotely. Some make the drive to work across the bay to Mobile, which I think is one of the most beautiful and interesting cities in America. We grab lunch with friends at a meat-n-three or sit in the park and pull out a sandwich that drips with tomatoes picked in our backyard the day before.

We take art, yoga, and acting classes and volunteer at the hospital, museum, school, or church. We buy ice cream cones for our children at Mr. Gene's Beans, then let them run around in the correctly named Fairhoper's Community Park.

If we feel strongly about a cause (which is almost always), we organize a group to help. Families in need? Birdhouse projects? Public park beautification? Consider it done.

On Friday nights, you'll find us downtown for Art Walk or at the high school football stadium awaiting the earth-shaking boom of the pirate cannon that, for miles around, frightens dogs, rattles windows, and terrifies the other team's players to the point we've seen them hit the ground thinking there's an incoming attack.

Our kids swim, our hounds howl, the mullet jump, and the pelicans glide. Parades roll, shrimp boil, and funerals hurt. We laugh, complain, cry, and love. Then, we are eager to climb into bed at night because we know we'll get to do it all again the next day. There will be flowers to pick for the dinner table, cakes to bake for new neighbors, prayers to be lifted for the sick, gifts to wrap for new babies, and another sunset over Mobile Bay that will leave us breathless.

No matter what you call us, we are blessed and loved, and life is good for Fairhopers.

3

Hey, Don't Push!

Here's what happened.

In the fall of 2015, I was writing a weekly newspaper column for Gulf Coast Media Newspapers and posting stories on my blog. Little did I know that a chance encounter with a woman who lacked social graces would launch my readership into new heights and serve as a conversation starter for the entire community.

Sometimes you have to experience the bad before you recognize the good. This is where the bad part all began. But don't worry, I'll tell you all about the good later.

One night in a small town

The blocked-off downtown streets buzzed with excitement as the annual "Lighting of the Trees" event began. Held every November, just before Thanksgiving, it was a sweet way to usher in the holiday season. News sources reported that the previous year's crowd was around 6,000 people, but this year, in 2015, the attendance ballooned to at least double if not more. The larger than usual crowd took the city officials off guard.

It was a tradition to gather in the barricaded streets to listen to performers sing and play music, then like a gathering of NASA enthusiasts, everyone would count down, 10 – 9 – 8. . . , until we hit "zero!" and suddenly, downtown Fairhope was awash in millions of twinkling lights in the trees that lined the streets. Mrs. Claus arrived from the North Pole in time to sit in a tiny house where she could talk with the children. It was a breathtaking sight that made even the most cold-hearted Scrooge catch his breath in awe.

At first, the larger than normal crowd was only a problem for those trying to find parking spaces. One friend texted me and said she and her husband had turned around to go back home without ever getting out of their cars because the traffic was so bad. What was going on?

Usually, a small-town vibe was in the air as schoolchildren lined the streets, some years displaying their class projects. People milled about, calling out across the street to each other, as most people we saw were familiar. But 2015 was the axis of change, and for the first time ever, we felt the squeeze of an uncomfortable and totally unfamiliar situation.

After the lights had been turned on and the large crowd began to leave, we were caught in a human traffic jam. We felt like sardines, packed tightly against a building on one side and a stalled mass of people on the other. The crowd became wall-to-wall human statues who couldn't move. This was something new to small-town folks.

Trapped in a small space, my husband, Bob, who was standing on my left, reached over and took my hand because he knows I get anxious in crowds, and he's just nice that way. What a guy.

Everyone was frustrated, yet calmly chatted about the evening, when suddenly a woman barged through the crowd and pushed her way to stand on my right. She bumped several of us, and as we wobbled back and forth, she wedged herself into a spot until she could go no further. Angry that people were in her way, she yelled, "Move it, people! Let me through!"

The gentleman in front of us politely turned his head toward us and calmly said, "We're all trying to go in the same direction, ma'am."

His gentle reply did nothing to quiet her. She responded by screaming at the back of his head, "Well, you need to move your feet then!"

At that point, everyone strained their necks to get a look at this abrasive person. I was embarrassed to be standing next to her. What if someone thought she was my friend? I love friends who are loud and fun, but this woman was loud and rude, which is not my friend style at all.

"Push!" she barked, then repeated even louder, "Shove, just shove!"

I tried speaking calmly to her to see if I could reduce the tension. She engaged for a brief moment and told me she was from a nearby small town. I tried the old standby of talking about the weather. She only took a deep breath and bellowed, "Everybody, push!" "PUSH!"

At that moment, something inside me snapped, and in a calm but firm tone, I looked at her and said, "We don't push in Fairhope."

Even my straight-talking husband from New Jersey gasped at my boldness. He squeezed my hand and seemed poised to come to my defense, but guess what? It worked. The woman became silent, and after a few awkward minutes that seemed like hours, the crowd finally shuffled around the corner to where we never saw her again. I was shaking like a tin roof in a hurricane.

Hold on while I write this down

What do people do when something good, bad, happy, or sad happens, and they aren't writers? I love communicating through the written word, yet lean heavily on the visual cues that accompany Southern verbal communication like hand motions, finger snaps, and hair flips to help get the point across. It isn't easy to type an eye roll.

So, I did what came naturally: I went home after the Tree Lighting fiasco and wrote it all down in an animated and highly descriptive blog post. I didn't submit the story as a weekly newspaper column because I didn't think many people would find it interesting, but boy, was I ever wrong! (Insert an eye-rolling finger snap here.)

On my computer, I told the story of the woman who frightened the bee jibbers out of me by encouraging a stampede. I had seen footage of out-of-control soccer games in foreign countries where stadiums collapsed, and bulls ran through the streets, causing tsunamis and killing thousands of innocent people. Okay, the exact details were a blur, but I did know that a pushing and shoving crowd could be a very dangerous thing.

When I had taught school, I often used "we" statements to remind children that their actions affected others. "We don't throw blocks," or "We share the paints." It worked so well I also used it with my two sons. "We don't talk like that in our family," and "We don't watch those kinds of movies." The message of "we" can be powerful, except I do hate it when the waiter asks, "What will *we* be having tonight?"

Once a teacher, always a teacher, and once a mother to boys, you don't put up with much "crud." When this woman behaved like a kindergartener, throwing a temper tantrum, I wasn't going to stand for it.

"We don't push in Fairhope" resonated with the entire town and far beyond.

Readers of my blog immediately shared the story, and *The Mobile Press-Register* ended up writing their own story about my blog post on the front page of their pre-Thanksgiving Day issue. Front page? Yes, ma'am. Front and center in the big fat edition with all the Black Friday coupons. My blog post about the pushing woman was big-time.

Suddenly, everyone was saying, "We don't push in Fairhope."

My intent was for the story to be about someone who used bad manners. Everyone else interpreted it as a story about uncontrolled city growth. Either way, I didn't regret saying it one bit.

This is getting crazy

The Press-Register's social media department put a "teaser" headline on the Facebook link to their newspaper story in order to gain more traffic and clicks from readers — but that's their job, so I understood, although I thought it was a bit unfair. I had to remember that "headlines make the story." Their click-bait caption was, "If you're heading to Fairhope, remember they don't like pushy outsiders."

"Well, that's not what I said at all," I told Bob. "You're getting new readers by the truckload, just go with it," he told me.

What I thought was a commentary on social etiquette turned into hot discussion about all the old buildings being knocked down, the new houses being built, and the traffic jams on the four-lane. I'd stepped into a big mess.

I was painted as an inhospitable villain by many who only glanced at the "pushy outsiders" headline and didn't bother to read the story before they commented. I began to worry about the reading comprehension skills of many commenters. Those who took the time to read my full story had only positive things to say and agreed with me, whether they lived here or not.

A friend called and said, "They're talking about you on the radio!" I didn't even have time to find a radio, so I ran outside, sat in the car, and listened to the Midday Mobile show. Popular talk show host Sean Sullivan was discussing my story with another guest, and they were completely missing the point, focusing instead on how mean and closed-minded people in Fairhope must be. I couldn't stand it anymore, so I called the station and said, "Um, this is the actual author of the story. Wouldn't you like to speak directly with me?" After a quick commercial break, I was on-air, discussing the growth problem of our area and repeating, "We love visitors but want everyone to be nice." Although I could quote Miss Manners forward and back, they somehow thought I should also know city zoning and planning regulations. Thank goodness I was a quick study on the highlights of city issues, because this went on for months.

When the story went viral, I spoke with the editor at Alabama Media Group, who owned the *Mobile Press-Register*, and said, "Your writers are writing stories about my stories. Don't you think I should be writing for you?" He agreed, and I spent the next seven years writing a weekly lifestyle column for the Mobile, Birmingham, and Huntsville newspapers. Even though my columns were usually related to Southern topics, my work was occasionally syndicated in newspapers in Syracuse, New York, and Grand Rapids, Michigan, where I gained many wonderful followers.

People of all ages, all over town, were calling out to me, "We don't push in Fairhope!" It was a slogan for defending our way of life and was whispered to me in church, yelled across parking lots, and tossed out as I entered restaurants. It became a cheer of unity and a battle cry for small-town preservation. A few months later, a Mardi Gras float passed by, and as the masked man tossed me beads, he laughed and shouted, "We don't push in Fairhope!" It seemed I had broken the dam of thoughts already churning in everyone's minds. "What's happening to our small town?"

Hey, Don't Push!

When they push my casket down in the grave someday, I'm sure some smarty-pants will mutter, "Ha! I guess we do push in Fairhope." I'll answer by haunting them for the rest of their lives.

Did we live happily ever after?

My blog post received several hundred comments and the *Press-Register* social media page received thousands. Almost all were supportive of the story, but a few were like this:

"You are dumb and there's nothing good to eat or buy in Fairhope."

Most said things like:

"Very well put! Thank you for addressing what is a concern to many locals. I've grown up here and so has my husband. After the lighting of the trees, my husband and I both said that would be it. We, along with our children, could barely get from one side of the street to the other! We came home irritable and exhausted from what was once a relaxing family experience. Something needs to be done to keep our sweet town from being destroyed."

Some said I should be writing about terrorism or the poor, but this guy won the prize for the most original thought and inventive spelling:

"If people wanna come let them come!! Jesus didn't turn away anybody who came to him he loved everybody. Your like the parents keeping the children away from Jesus, but Jesus loves all the little children wether they are red, yellow, black, or white. Yes I know I just quoted the song. You gotta love people whether they are from Fairhope or not."

My reply was:

"I'm 'keeping children from Jesus'?
Wow.
Whether or not you care, You're welcome."

And thank goodness for my regular readers, who "get me":

"And some people can find humor in everything, may they be blessed. Leslie Anne, you make me cry laughing. Absolutely love you!"

I promise, that wasn't from my mother.

Journalist John Sharp from the *Press-Register* wrote a question and answer–style article and interviewed the Fairhope mayor, who commented that he didn't see any problem with the crowd that night and added that I probably had my feelings hurt. He was replaced in the next election in favor of a mayor and city council that campaigned on the promise to control growth. But would we see results?

Two of the questions John asked me were:

Press Register: Are there any concerns you might have that the reaction (to your blog post) might fuel perceptions in Baldwin County (and elsewhere) that Fairhope residents can be pretentious?

Tarabella: Since when did wanting everyone to have good manners make you pretentious? It's two entirely different things, although nowadays, many folks think it's their right to misbehave in public and think everyone else should just "deal with it." Very few people took away a pretentious tone from the story, but if they did, I think they weren't regular readers of mine and only got their information from a snippet on Facebook and didn't take the time to read the entire story.

Press Register: What do you hope, personally, comes out of the blog post and the reaction from it?

Tarabella: As a writer, it's always fun to have a large audience, but I also want to use my work to entertain and help people. This unexpected discussion about the future of our county, and even our entire region is obviously on the forefront of people's minds. If this has sparked that conversation, then I'm happy. Only good things can come from intelligent discussion and planning.

In my haste of writing the blog post, I inadvertently offended some by reporting the pushy woman had said she was from nearby Robertsdale. I truly love the neighboring community of Robertsdale, but my wording made a few people think I was demeaning it by calling it a "farming community." Coming from me, the granddaughter of a county agent, that was meant to be a compliment. I added that everyone else I'd ever met from there was wonderful. Then, I said that if our growth continued at such a wild, unorganized pace, we could "end up like (gasp) Orlando." A woman wrote and defended that strip mall–infested city by pointing to their lovely old downtown area. I profusely apologized to the kind people of Robertsdale but stuck to my guns on Orlando.

An interesting side story is that in the weeks following this post, two separate women sent me emails, confessing to being the woman who tried to start the stampede. "I was the woman you told not to push," said one. The other also insisted she was the guilty pusher. Clues in each of their notes let me know both were lying. They got the location and a few other details wrong. But for the life of me, I can't understand why anyone would want to be labeled as the one who encouraged a madhouse trampling event. This is a very strange world, indeed.

In the following years, the city workers wisely installed a second stage to distribute the tree-lighting festivities throughout the entire downtown area and encouraged new parking areas in all directions. Other nearby municipalities began to hold their own celebrations, so the crowds were manageable.

The best thing that came from this story, other than my long-time column with Advance Publication Newspapers, was in the following years, people seemed more aware of being kind and helping those who had mobility issues. People took the reminder to heart and behaved with compassion.

That year, our small-town event doubled from the previous year's 6,000 attendees to a whopping 12,000. This past year, in 2023, Fox 10 News reported there were between 30,000 and 40,000 in attendance. But no one pushed.

Mission accomplished.

It was a challenge to leave Prattville, the place where I grew up and loved. My salvation was in the beauty of Fairhope. Driving to my office in Mobile, the light over Mobile Bay was like diamonds sparkling on the water. It was 1983 and Fairhope was still a small town.
— **Barbara S. Wheeler**, Representative, Alabama Silver-Haired Legislature

4

How Did You Get Here?

All behind you hushes and fades as you slip through the hedge. What lies ahead is sparkling with colors and sounds so surreal you can't quite believe what you see. Pterodactyl-like birds skim the surface of the water against a sky that appears to be a movie set. You tip your head to avoid brushing the soft fringe of moss dangling from twisted trees. Stepping around the gemstone flowerbeds, you overhear people who seem to be just a bit too friendly — they must want something and should be avoided. Yet after deeply inhaling both blossom and beach, then rubbing your eyes, you finally realize everything is real. Congratulations, you've discovered Fairhope.

Or, maybe you just stopped for gas and a Slim Jim somewhere on Highway 98.

No matter what brought you here, many will say they somehow "stumbled upon" this place by accident.

"I was there to attend my roommate's wedding." "We were on our way to the beach and stopped to eat." "I had a meeting at the Grand Hotel." "I remembered reading a story about Fairhope in the *Atlanta Journal-Constitution* and decided to grab lunch there on my way to New Orleans."

It doesn't matter how you found Fairhope; everyone who was meant to be here eventually finds their way.

But the stories have recently shifted from someone popping through the hedge now and then to more of a roaring tidal wave. Like a party when your parents left town, one invited another, then he told his friends, and before you realized it, 23 people were packed into the kitchen eating leftover meatloaf and squirting chocolate syrup into their mouths.

The understatement of the last decade is "things have changed."

Predictably, some bucolic fields have been replanted with porch-less and soul-less houses, and roads are now paved where there was once red dirt. Some newcomers irritatingly demanded we change and do things like they did "back home," but they didn't realize the real change, yet to come, was for them.

How Did You Get Here?

Little by little, the sunsets worked a hypnotic trance while the salty air triggered deep, slow breaths. The common speed limit of 25 mph, and in some places a slothful 15, slowed them down a bit. Sipping coffee began to be a ritual observed around a table in the local coffee shop where the barista knew their order as they walked in the door, not something they gulped down in gridlock. Church wasn't something lost on their childhood as they rediscovered friendly families of faith. New friends encouraged them to dust off an old hobby or finally pursue their dream of singing with the community choral society. We watched as they didn't change Fairhope as much as Fairhope changed them.

The country folks and country club folks started a book club, and the Catholics and Presbyterians took art classes with their Jewish neighbors. The white and blue collars discussed the news over scrambled eggs at Julwin's while the Democrats square-danced with the Republicans. It wasn't as intimate as when the founders of Fairhope skinny-dipped together in the bay, but it's close enough for now.

Not everyone likes Fairhope enough to remain here forever, and that's okay. It's not everyone's cup of tea. Some leave to follow jobs, love, or adventure. They told us they absolutely had to have better pizza, art, bagels, schools, theatre, traffic jams, or smog. We blew them a kiss and wished them well.

Truth be told, the people who fled are correct. Fairhope lacks quite a few things. Some boast that the school rankings are at the top of the state but ignore the fact that Alabama bounces around at the bottom of the barrel. The same is true for shopping, restaurants, and entertainment. Like most small towns, we're good, but not in the running for world-class greatness, unless you count that little ol' James Beard Award nomination The Hope Farm received.

People are often surprised to learn the best parties of the year are the Rotary Steak Cook-Off and Piggly Wiggly's Taste of Lower Alabama. Living here has its trade-offs. Some are irritated by the majority's loyalty to "guns, God, and grits," but they must remember that at the end of the day, they're resting their heads in Sweet Home, way down South, Alabama. So far, it's a peaceful co-existence because everyone understands where and who we are and knows the road into town also leads out. Most here were also raised to behave themselves, with the emphasis on "most."

But for those who stay, Fairhope is like an old pair of jeans. It doesn't matter if they're tattered or even outdated. For some, Fairhope is the perfect fit that feels just right.

Fairhope has more flowers than dogs, more dogs than people, and more people than good sense. Our passions sometimes overshadow the obvious practical paths, but it makes for a good story, and stories are the literal foundation on which Fairhope was built.

How Did You Get Here?

Among all the necessary supplies the founders brought with them in 1894 was a printing press. They believed their story of a Single Tax Colony should be documented and shared. Written communication was valued, and their newspaper, *The Fairhope Courier*, was circulated before they even arrived on the Eastern Shore of Mobile Bay. "The Courier" was where I wrote my first weekly column for three years, so I feel connected to those storytelling pioneers.

Although 75 percent of what I'll tell you about Fairhope can also apply to the rest of the South, there's still something else that makes this town unique. Sure, grits are grits in Fairhope or Valdosta, and Spanish moss dangles from trees here but can also be found in Savannah. So, what is this uniqueness that sets us apart? If you awoke from a deep sleep and looked around, how would you know you weren't in Slidell, Tallahassee, or Wetumpka? Things are changing all over the South, in Ocean Springs, DeFuniak Springs, and Sawyerton Springs, yet Fairhope's originality springs eternal.

If we share 75 percent of our characteristics with other places, then what's in that other 25 percent — or maybe more — that makes us uniquely "Fairhope"?

Our uniqueness can be found in unseasonably warm days when a lady wearing orange polka dot boots fans herself with the 24 thank-you notes she's dropping at the post office before walking up the hill, where the librarian wearing a flamingo hat helps her find a book about Clay City Tiles, and as she carries the book home, sees traffic stopped for parading wrinkly shar-peis being pulled in homemade spaceships, which reminds her she needs to press her dress for church the next day, but relaxes, knowing her deviled eggs are already fixed in the refrigerator for the fifth Sunday dinner, then as she turns onto Section Street, feels the weather suddenly switch to a bone-chilling wind and hopes her husband remembered to pick up the three pounds of shrimp for gumbo after he helped the neighbor prune his satsuma tree.

Those are 100 percent Fairhope days.

We're not everyone's cup of tea, and even the locals are often discontented with one thing or the other, but those who manage to slip through the hedge and find their place to belong are the happy ones, for they have found home.

5

Reverse Seinfeld

One of my all-time favorite television series is Seinfeld, although I didn't fully understand one of the first episodes I ever saw when the characters Kramer, George, Elaine, and Jerry were lost in a parking garage. They couldn't remember where they parked and therefore spent the entire show wandering around in search of their car. "How could they lose their car?" I wondered. It didn't make any sense until I finally grasped that New York City parking garages are far more expansive than any of the small parking structures I'd ever seen. When I traveled to large cities, it was usually by plane and I took taxis, so I didn't need to park. The two largest cities I had lived in were the (then), medium-sized towns of Tallahassee, Florida, and Marietta, Georgia, which at the time, didn't require me to park in anything other than a flat Kroger grocery store lot.

Leslie Anne Tarabella

My confusion of not understanding a large city will probably be reversed for some of you reading these stories. If you've only lived in large towns, especially outside of the Southern United States, you may have trouble relating to some of these places with their quirky and unique issues and people.

I recently lamented to friends that Fairhope was getting a new Starbucks. "Oh! I love Starbucks," said one, who lived in a large town in New Jersey and traveled to big cities quite often. "I like being able to get off the interstate and grab a cup of coffee," said the other, who was from Atlanta and also traveled extensively. I tried to explain, "But we're ten miles from the interstate and already have several locally owned coffee shops, owned by friends we like to support." The two looked thoughtful for a moment as if they tried to envision a morning of grabbing coffee from a small-town Alabama shop. "Hmm," was all they had to say after that. They aren't alone. Many who have moved here from big cities are celebrating the arrival of large chain grocery stores, coffee shops, and more. A hotly debated topic last summer was, "What's the plural of 'Publix'?" (We now have three, all within two miles of my house.) These people want to live in a small town, yet want to bring the big comforts with them.

Yes, it's often inconvenient to live in a small community. We're accustomed to everything closing by 8 p.m., driving a long way to the airport, not being able to buy the trendiest kinds of gadgets, and having to

Reverse Seinfeld

park a few blocks away to get our cup of coffee instead of sitting in a drive-thru line. But by doing so, our store owners get to spend time with their families, and we get to talk to other people and have the clerk ask about our son. When we walk down the street to get our coffee, we can smell the flowers planted on the corners. And I've never once lost my car in our compact downtown parking garage.

As for the big-city Seinfeld characters? They met their sad jailhouse series ending when they passed through a small town in Massachusetts and didn't quite understand that town's slower way of life. I don't think we'll resort to locking people up who want to sip a name-brand cup of coffee, but after slurping a month's worth of expensive high-calorie mocha chip Frappuccinos with chocolate drizzle and cream, they may be inspired to start walking down the street to grab a cup of joe from the mom-and-pop shop.

The Dogwood Trail Court serves as goodwill ambassadors for the Eastern Shore of Baldwin County.

6

The Truth About Newcomers

The truth is, Fairhopers love the new people they meet.

The end.
Move on, nothing more to say.

P.S.

Oh, but wait. I thought of something else. Everyone especially loves when the new folks join in and connect with our activities. Their enthusiasm for their new home reminds us how good it is here, and we love "most"—well, "some"—okay, "a few" of the ideas they bring. No, we aren't going to do it like you did "back home." This is your home now, so get in the South Alabama groove. (And there's no need to shout.)

When people willingly choose to move to a new place, it's because they want to be there, not because they feel obligated to stay close to the old homestead where great-granddaddy once planted that tree — right over there. Yes, that's the one, being chopped down now for progress.

Those who were required to relocate here due to job changes are often grumpy at first, thinking they've been transferred to the middle of a bad episode of *Hee Haw* (if there is such a thing). But once they stay a while, they understand we won't force them to participate in Bible drills and oyster-eating contests or to join the ukulele band (it's all completely voluntary). Then they begin to relax and notice the good things (and there's no need to blow that horn).

On a recent visit to the Fairhope Museum of History, I found most docents to be retired newcomers. They have the time and passion to tell others about the city they chose to love. Truth be told, those who have been here for several generations often grow tired of doing everything and welcome others who are willing to step in and help. The library volunteers, Hospital Auxiliary, and Welcome Center are also heavily staffed by "new" people in town, and we are grateful.

The Truth About Newcomers

We actually have an official "Newcomer's Club," and it's so much fun that several of their members have lived in Fairhope for at least 20 years but refuse to relinquish their membership.

The fast track for instant acceptance can be found in your ancestry; if you are descended from a former Miss Alabama, SEC football star, or governor (incarcerated or not), you'll be welcomed with fanfare. I found my sweet spot as a descendant of one of the 13 Ghosts of Alabama, made popular by the late author Kathryn Tucker Windham. It helps to have a past with a hook, or in this case, a haint.

My rule, which I'd love to make into law, is that for every lovely new person who moves into town, one other resident can be voted out. It's population control at a basic level. Most days, there are only two or three on my "vote out" list, perhaps a few more just after I've attended a poorly run meeting that could have been handled by email.

If we removed all the restaurants, shops, events, and projects that were initiated or staffed by "newcomers," people who moved here either 70 years ago or 7 months ago, our city would be very bland.

Sandra Bishop is one of my favorite longtime Fairhopers, whom I would have sworn was born and raised here. Honored to be the first homecoming queen at Fairhope High School and a majorette with the marching band, Sandra moved from Illinois to Fairhope at the beginning of her high school years and stole the heart of Clarence, whom she later married; together, they raised a lovely family. They have successfully operated B&B Pecans for decades, making it a necessity for holiday baking and gift-giving traditions.

Most newcomers appreciate the same things everyone else likes and fuss about the same issues long-timers do, like increased traffic, urban sprawl, and people who push.

Bless their hearts; they're just like us, after all. No wonder we love them.

7

Meanwhile, in the Coffee Shop

As Mattie Mae slid into her chair, she got straight to the point and said, "Y'all, they're painting nekkid people at the Art Center."

Marybeth's eyes popped wide as she said, "Wouldn't that tickle?"

Velda, who had married well and divorced even better, snorted as she sipped her iced coffee through the straw.

"I declare!" said Sandra as she tapped another sugar pack into her coffee. "I don't know what in the cat hair is going on in Fairhope anymore. Parties all night, children zipping around wild as a rip in golf carts, and now bare butts at the Art Center?"

"When can I sign up?" Marybeth wanted to know. "Seriously, is there still room in this class?"

"It's the Hollywood people showing up to make movies that's making everybody crazy," reasoned Mattie Mae. "They bring a certain vibe to town, and we all know what kind of vibe that is." Twisting her mouth to one side, she whispered, "The movie stars who come here are on my prayer list; bless their hearts."

Marybeth laughed and said, "Yeah, but there are some clean-as-a-whistle movies being filmed here, too, so you can't blame the famous folks. I saw that tall, good-looking guy, Jason; what was his name?"

"Segel!" said two others in unison.

". . . in the Piggly Wiggly, and he was just as nice as could be. Kelsey Grammer was here right after that, and I lost my mind and hollered out, "Hey, Frasier!"

"Well, I'm hoping Harry Connick Jr. will come to Fairhope to make a movie. Who knows? He may pop in on an art class while he's here." Marybeth blushed at the thought.

"What is it with you and Harry Connick Jr.?"

Meanwhile, in the Coffee Shop

"Oh, hush up," Marybeth told them. "You know he's hot as a pistol."

"Y'all are deranged. Artists have been sketching figures since bodies were first invented. Haven't you ever traveled and seen paintings of beautiful people hanging in the museums in Europe? Y'all are so small-town," fussed Velda.

"I guess when you dwell on it for a while, it's really a celebration of creation," said Marybeth. "After all, think about the Sistine Chapel and all the bare-bottom babies flying around. If it's good enough for the Vatican, then Fairhope is in good company."

"You always were a hippie," Mattie Mae said as she poked her in the arm. Scrunching up her nose, she added, "Yeah, I actually think a lot of those paintings are lovely, but it's just weird having that sort of thing going on here. I mean, who do they get to model? What if you showed up for a class and found your neighbor buck-nekkid? Well, I'll tell ya, I'd just up and die."

"I'd barf," said Sandra, "cause y'all know who my neighbor is." All the ladies pretended to gag, and two added, "Eww!" "Oh my gosh, that man is meaner than a hot skillet of rattlesnakes." Velda nearly spat out her coffee at the thought and said, "And lordymighty, he's ugly."

"Fairhope's more open-minded than most people know," said Sandra as she finished her coffee. "We're just polite enough to keep it on the down low. There's no need to run around and tell everyone what we're up to. You know, ugly names, ugly faces always seen in public places."

"It's because our mamas taught us better," laughed Marybeth as all the others nodded in agreement. Sandra cracked up, saying, "Yeah, but they also taught us to keep our britches on in public."

Still laughing, Velda said, "I need to run."
"Already? Oh, stay a little longer," the others insisted.

Velda smiled, slung her backpack over her shoulder, and called out, "Can't. I'm late for class."

8

18 Rules

New to town? The "N.F.C." (New Folk Committee), a subcommittee of the larger "Committee for the Preservation of Loveliness," has issued a few helpful guidelines for fitting into town.

1. Jump in and help. You moved here because you love our parades and festivals, so get involved. We want to get to know you and need your help.

2. Don't complain about the line at the post office. Enjoy the wait while you smile at other people. But remember, in the South, a smile is just a smile. Flirting is a separate issue your mama should have taught you about. Don't worry, you'll know it when it hits you.

3. Get ready to have someone invite you to visit their church. We aren't judging your values or spirituality, it's just what we do when we like you. Churches are important parts of the community, and we simply want to share the joy (but don't sit in our pew).

4. Get to know the local architects — they don't bite. We have many gorgeous homes, old and new, but make sure you fit into your surroundings. That 9,000-square-foot modern-farmhouse-teepee you built in the middle of two 1,000-square-foot historic coastal cottages will get you discussed.

5. Don't ever be discussed.

6. Shop in locally owned stores. Like the safety sign that says, "24 days without an accident," we boast, "65 days without visiting a chain store." It won't remain special unless we support unique (and her sister Monique).

7. "Fruit and Nut" is not a commentary on your personality, although I do have a few nutty friends who live there. It's okay, it's their badge of honor.

8. Only beep your car horn if you're saying, "Hey there, buddy!" If someone cuts you off in traffic, you should whisper a sincere, "Bless his heart." Then say a little prayer that he's not rushing to the hospital. It goes

without saying, "We don't honk in Fairhope." We also pull over for funeral processions. If you don't, you'll be hit upside the head with rule #5.

9. Please don't tell our children they don't need to say yes, ma'am, and no sir (or thank you and please). We raised them that way for a reason, and it's not your job to change them.

10. Satsumas. Know them, grow them, eat them, share them.

11. You're not really a true Fairhoper until Donnie Barrett or Cecil Christenberry knows your name. You can't go wrong having either one as a friend.

12. Always keep a box or bag in the back of your car just in case you catch the Flower Fairies (aka the public works landscaping crew), who will share the pruned blossoms and discarded bulbs with you.

13. At some point, you'll want to get a bow for your mailbox. We put bows on everything, including our children, doors, trees, and little dogs. We once "yarn bombed" the entire town with crocheted tree and light post decorations. If your little girl doesn't wear a hair bow, go back to #5.

14. We like to match the flowers, so wear bright colors. Save the all-black for grieving or evening.

15. It's considered bad form to knock little children down for Mardi Gras beads. But everyone is on their own and all decency is discarded if a MoonPie is launched in your direction.

16. If Fairhope is ever in the running for a "best of" contest, all the locals secretly vote against it (oh, give me a break, you know it's true). I always vote for Beaufort.

17. No matter how much it kills you, don't ever begin a sentence with, "We did it better back in . . ."

18. Regarding #5, sometimes it's fun to be discussed, but don't worry. In five minutes, they'll move on to someone else.

9

A Fair Hope of Success

Hope is gentle enough to encourage new love yet bold enough to send soldiers into war. Hope is rooted in a spiritual context and used when rolling the dice.

If I'd had a little girl, there's a big chance that if not named "Ruby Diamond," she would have been named "Hope" because it has always been my favorite word and a concept I've thought about quite a bit. "Hope" is only one skip away from "home," which is yet another single syllable of warmth.

When I took Italian lessons, I heard *speranza* and thought it was a beautiful word even before I learned it translated to "hope." In any language, hope seems to be a lovely thought.

The saddest phrase in the world is, "There is no hope."

I've never believed it was possible to be hopeless. Even if a doctor, lawyer, or mechanic says there's no hope, I always think God knows more and is the God of hope who never abandons his children. Where there is God, there is hope. Some would say that's being a dreamy optimist, while others understand it's faith.

With my hopeful heart, it's no wonder I've found my home in a place entwined with the pursuit of dreams and hope. The founders selected "Fairhope" because it specifically reflected their dream of establishing a city with a "fair hope" of success. They left their homes in Iowa for their Utopia in Alabama and saw their hopes of a Single Tax Colony realized. Even though they were dreamers, I doubt any of them dared to dream of the magnitude of beauty, growth, and popularity we enjoy today.

With their provisions of horses, lumber, books, and a printing press, they also brought hearts bursting with so much hope they must have awakened in the middle of the night, too excited to sleep, thinking of the great adventure ahead.

A Fair Hope of Success

Their hope was mixed with dreams and the secret ingredient — creativity — which some say is found in the Fairhope water.

The founders held great hope in a city that overlooked a beautiful bay where residents could create new ways to educate, live, worship, celebrate, and enjoy life. In 1894, the hearts of our founders held an abundance of hope. The plans for their experimental city indeed had a "fair hope" of success.

I hope that the dreamers, schemers, and lovers remain in Fairhope forever.

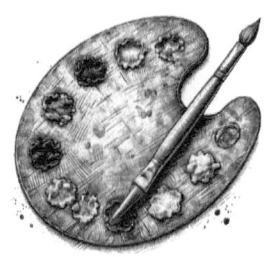

You came here from there because you didn't like it there, and now you want to change here to be like there. You are welcome here, only don't try to make here like there. If you want to make here like there, you shouldn't have left there in the first place.
Social Media Post

10

Operation Home Sweet Home

Home is where the heart is, and in 2022, Fairhopers were reminded that sometimes exceptional hearts call for exceptional homes.

Smitten with her beautiful blonde hair, John fell in love with Krystal in their special needs kindergarten class at the Fairhope K-1 Center. They eventually attended different schools, but John always remembered his childhood friend.

Living with his parents in a downtown house that first belonged to his grandmother, John would walk to Panini Pete's, a popular Fairhope lunch spot, and hang out to watch the bustling activity of the restaurant. The staff welcomed the curious teenager and gave him a cool drink on hot days. John started greeting guests and busing tables without being asked. Owner Pete

Blohme, who operates several restaurants in Mobile and Fairhope and is also a guest chef on The Food Network, said, "I figured I'd start paying him because we loved having him around, and then, he just kind of stayed."

John admired the busy entrepreneur, and as the mentor relationship grew, it inspired Pete to partner with his friend Robert Kabakoff to form a charitable foundation that aids the special-needs population, veterans, and no-kill animal shelters. Pete explained, "The P.R. Foundation is a direct result of my friendship with John."

Because true love always finds a way, John and Krystal reunited and found their kindergarten crush was now real love. They married in a simple ceremony at First Baptist Church of Fairhope and held the reception at Panini Pete's. Sadly, John's parents had passed away, and friends realized the family house, where the young couple planned to live, was in disrepair.

Patched floors and walls were only a temporary solution to a worsening problem. With no family to help, it seemed hopeless.

But anything is possible when you live in a city founded on hope.

John's former high school principal, Beverly Thomas, and teacher, Tina McGough, met with Pete. After a home inspection, the group received the overwhelming news that the house would have to be entirely demolished. The only solution was to rebuild from the ground up.

Although this is the kind of project Pete's new P.R. Foundation was designed to tackle, the organization was still in the early stages of development, and they knew they needed help to address a project of this magnitude. This monumental undertaking would need a miracle. "I knew there had to be a way to make this work," said Pete.

John was part of the Panini Pete's family. His connections to people throughout town made him a friend to everyone he met. Spending his days in the restaurant, John also ventured around town to make lunch deliveries on a unique adult-sized tricycle equipped with a large basket for orders. His friend Mike Lyons, owner of the nearby Lyon's Share Art Gallery, helped John create a fun daily video listing the restaurant's specials.

Pete explained, "John's presence at Panini Pete's changed my life and the lives of the restaurant's team members. He also had a great effect on the customers and everyone in town. John grew the muscle in all of us, which makes us want to give and do more for others. We felt so strongly about this project; we were prepared to take the financial risk if no one else stepped in."

For better or worse, news travels fast in Fairhope, and soon everyone in town was talking about "John's house." The city, full of hope, sprang into action for "Operation Home Sweet Home."

Custom home designer Christina Stankowski offered to design the perfect cottage for the couple. Other donations began pouring in, and fundraisers were held. Excitement built — quite literally — when The Baldwin County Homebuilder's Association Charitable Foundation offered its full support. With so many resources falling into place, it felt like the entire town was swept up in a beautiful holiday movie.

Donations of materials and work began to pour in. Decorators, furniture stores, private individuals, and church members pitched in to help. Kitchen appliances, flooring, cabinetry, heating and cooling, and landscaping were donated to create a dream-come-true house for the sweet couple. Back at his restaurants, Pete sold his popular beignet mixes and T-shirts to raise additional funds. After their regular jobs, volunteers often arrived at the construction site late in the day to begin work. Tractors, cement trucks, and electrical vans lined up day after day for what felt like the most heartfelt parade in town.

Nearly a year later, on a chilly February day in 2023, with hearts pounding and tears of joy streaming down cheeks, the community gathered on the front lawn of the new two-bedroom, two-bath house to welcome the young couple home. The Fairhope High School pep band played on the front lawn, and John and Krystal arrived in a golf cart to cut the ribbon draping the front porch. Speeches were hurried because no one wanted to delay the homecoming a minute longer than necessary. After months of hard work and dreaming, John and Krystal finally walked through the door of their beautiful new home. The looks on their faces reflected amazement, joy, and gratitude.

The charming cottage-style home fits perfectly into the neighboring area, close enough for John to walk to work at Panini Pete's. To this day, the house is kept neat as a pin. As a proud new homeowner, John was recently awaiting the delivery of his first lawnmower and looking forward to taking care of his very own yard.

The P.R. Foundation, which John originally inspired, will continue to spread goodness and hope throughout the community for many more years. John and Krystal can now grow old together in a safe and happy home, knowing the entire city cared enough to help in a time of need.

"Doing very special things for very special people" is the motto of the P.R. Foundation, and everyone agrees the sentiment is perfect. The residents of Fairhope made this home truly sweet. If you eat at Panini Pete's today, you'll find a delicious meal, good friends, and one of the happiest homeowners in town.

11

The Clock

Another day in Fairhope
begins as the sun glows on a soft field
of cotton. Katie's pedals grind as Cecil
chugs by and nods hello to the beat of WABF's
wake-up tunes, then Lori shares the news while crews
plant orangey marigolds. Squirrels scamper when Ashley's
heels tap staccato on the driveway and calls to Daisy, "Time to
visit the seniors." Marjorie sings, "Good morning" beneath the
fluttering red, white, and blue. Sputtering sprinklers spray and
office keys rattle. Pencils tap, pens click, computers whir,
paintbrushes splash. Sizzling shrimp and sweet beignets perfume
the air as old lovers shuffle down the pier while they dodge fishermen
flinging silver rings of net into the bay. The pastor snores until
awakened by the laughing ladies' flower guild. Sunny bus doors
flap as cheering children scamper into a whirling weekend of
imagination and the cheerleaders stretch before the game to
the beat of teen hearts on the drumline while pads clap
together on the illuminated field. Fans tromp up the
creaking bleachers to sit beneath a creamy vanilla
Moon Pie moon
to signal the clock to begin
another day in Fairhope.
tick
tock
tick
tock
tick
tock
tick
tock
tick
tock
tick
tock

As a newcomer to Alabama, you have to choose a side: Alabama or Auburn? As a newcomer to Fairhope, you're faced with an even worse drama: Ducks or feral cats?
— **JD Crowe**, political cartoonist for Alabama Media Group

12

The Post Office

It seems there's always a good story to be found at the Fairhope Post Office. Here's a note I jotted down for a future story in December 2019 after stopping to mail Christmas cards:

One lady in a Santa hat, one in a tiger hat, one in sparkly boots that made everyone shout, "We love your boots!" and one lady in polar bear tights. Everyone laughing and shouting, "Merry Christmas!" Last-minute Christmas cards? Stressful. Fairhope people? Lovely.

The Fairhope Post Office is where you can feel the pulse of the city. Sure, there are always a handful of stressed-out people who want to complain about standing in line, but for the most part, everyone is happy to be there. I've had issues with the accuracy of home delivery a few times — they seem to frown upon the box being full of cupcakes (it's the thought that counts, so thanks anyway , Barclay), but for the most part, going to the actual downtown post office is always a good experience.

For years, Mel worked behind the counter, and his cheerful demeanor and witty comments made mailing a package seem like a trip to the county fair with Doris Day tagging along. People almost looked for an excuse to stop by the post office as if it were happiness therapy.

But then, Mel retired (insert sad music here). And other delivery and shipping options emerged, so fewer people used the post office than in years past (more sad music, just for effect, goes here).

Others tried to fill Mel's shoes, and some did a pretty good job, but it was never the same. It's incredible how one person's positive outlook can have far-reaching tentacles throughout the entire town.

Recently, a new crew emerged behind the counter, and they made sending a letter happy again. No one will ever replace Mel, but the current gang will send you away with a smile. It isn't their job to spread joy, but being friendly is in their nature, and we're grateful.

In any city, you'll find a great blending of folks in the post office. Old friends greet each other, and children are excited to run into their teachers in the middle of the summer. Recipe tips are shared, and weather reports

The Post Office

are announced to no one in particular and to everyone listening. "Looks like a hurricane'll be here next week." "Says who?" "Says John Nodar on the TV, that's who."

But only some understand the camaraderie found at the post office. On what to us was a very "cold" day in Fairhope, I cracked my car windows open, locked the doors, and left my beagle, Lois Lane, inside to wait while I dashed in to drop off a package. Lois Lane was beautiful and smart. She knew if she pounced up and down on the steering wheel, the car alarm would sound, and I would come running back to her. As I closed the door, I looked into her amber eyes and instructed, "Do not touch the steering wheel!"

Standing in line, I watched out the window while Lois Lane bounced around, having a field day trying to locate the sweet spot, when a woman burst into the post office and screeched, "Someone left their dog in the car! Who would leave a dog in the car?" All polite chit-chat ceased, and in stunned silence, she stomped around some more and emphasized her message by waving her finger toward the parking lot as if we didn't remember where we parked our cars. Everyone in line realized it was a crisp and sunny 61 degrees, which to Southerners is downright frosty but lovely for our furry hounds. Many of us drive around with our dogs on pretty days, so no one said anything. Everyone just looked at her, a bit confused, and tried to figure out who she was.

I was enjoying the woman's show and had been writing a newspaper column long enough to realize if I let her keep fuming, she'd probably write that week's story for me. She kept on a-fussin' as everyone else avoided eye contact with her yet looked at one another with wry smiles. "Whoever is driving that white car had better go rescue that poor animal or I'm going to . . ." I finally spoke up, to save her from a stroke, and said it was my dog. "She likes running errands with me, and it's nice and cool today." Everyone in line nodded sympathetically at what I said. One gentleman I knew from the coffee shop said, "Oh, is Lois Lane in the car?"

And then, my car alarm went off.

After I slid the package across the counter, I sat in the car with the world's cutest beagle and had a word about her behavior. She didn't care a bit. As we were backing out of the parking lot, the woman, who still looked like a lemon eater, climbed into her big vehicle with a license tag from a faraway state. Lois Lane and I proceeded to the bookstore, where she found a bowl of water on the sidewalk, specifically placed there for precious pups. From there, we walked to the bank, where the teller gave Lois Lane a doggie treat and said, "I heard you were at the post office earlier today!" "Very funny," Lois thought.

With the influx of new residents from other parts of the country, the line at the post office isn't as chatty or friendly as in years past, but give them time. They'll come around.

The Post Office

The Fairhope Post Office is a great place to mail things, catch up with friends, and experience a bit of kindness, and it's an even better place to find a good story.

In Fairhope, gumbo's not just a soup, it's a way of life!
— **Malia Mullican**, Fairhope Native, cookbook author and food blogger at Little Coastal Kitchen

13

Served Up Right

When it comes to food, Fairhope is just your average Southern-coastal-farming-country-chic-gourmet-tourist-down-home sort of town. Whew! In other words, we aren't hurting for a delicious meal.

It's challenging to monitor our weight since living in the Bible Belt requires we wear the full armor of God, which has to add at least 10 pounds.

While sit-down family meals are fading from American culture, you can still find them in the South. It's often the only common experience family members share all day and a place where children learn the art of conversation. If a politician would campaign on the platform of mandating sit-down family suppers, he'd have my vote.

Grandmother's squash casserole, corn chowder, and seafood gumbo are always favorites along the Gulf Coast, not to mention cobbler for dessert made with blueberries picked that morning.

Sharing food is the way we love and care for one another, and the art of selecting the proper container for transporting the food can be as important and tricky as selecting the right lipstick for your wedding day. From recycled plastic butter tubs to fine china, there's a method to our madness and a purpose in choosing Tupperware or Tiffany for transporting the turnips.

Our favorite way of presenting a dish at a social event is in a pretty casserole dish, or even better, our mother's vintage Pyrex. At the gathering for a funeral luncheon, I admired Peggy's old Sandalwood Ivy Leaf Pyrex, and she said, "I wanted to make sure the table looked beautiful, because you know Weezie was such a dear to me. She would have appreciated the effort."

If someone in town doesn't have a proper casserole dish, it's a sign of deeper troubles and they'll be placed on the prayer list. It's the equivalent of not owning a toothbrush. How do you survive without one? Bless their hearts.

The most celebrated and useful invention since Miss Mississippi discovered hot rollers is the insulated casserole dish tote bag. It makes transporting a hot pan of pineapple casserole (the one Debbie makes with buttery Ritz Crackers on top) or sweet potato casserole (the one Barbara makes with gooey marshmallows on top) as easy as getting into community college.

Sometimes it's okay to use recycled or, nowadays, "eco-friendly" containers. I just delivered homemade soup to a friend in a Duke's Mayo jar — washed, with the label removed and a little blue ribbon tied 'round the top. The recipient was a man from church whose wife was in the hospital, and since men don't usually like to wash and return containers, it was the perfect soup vessel for him. Do you think he cared about the little blue ribbon? Of course not, but when he mentions it to his wife, she'll know we all took good care of him. Other times, your double recipe of Beyond the Grave Chicken Salad from Mary Kay Andrews warrants a lovely glass platter. As the popular Georgia author also suggested, "Yes, and don't forget to put a bit of lettuce on the plate for garnish — but not iceberg." Heavens, no. Arugula is the way to go.

The unofficial Tupperware of the South is the Cool Whip container. It's just the right size for delivering beef stew to your neighbor — but not the new neighbor. You have to get to know them first. New neighbors deserve something pretty. Once you become acquainted and catch their children picking your flowers and their noses, you can then send cookies in a plain old Ziploc bag.

Being a thoroughly Modern Millie, I favor the Pyrex company's later invention of CorningWare in the Cornflower Blue pattern. I've already inherited several pieces from my mother. It's vintage, but not so old that it's totally heartbreaking if chipped, which it never is. For some reason, good casserole dishes and fine china are like the ladies who own them. Classic, practical, and tougher than they look.

Showing up to some potluck dinners with a flimsy toss-away aluminum pan is wasteful, tacky, soulless, and a spill waiting to happen. They're seen as hostile to the environment and will make your hippie daughter-in-law cry. You must quickly soothe her by gifting her one of your mother's Gooseberry pattern Pyrex bowls. And really now, as Hippie Hannah points out, it only takes a minute to swish soapy water around the casserole dish and 42 years to decompose the foil pan. She's such a smart girl. Now, to teach her how to cook with meat.

Sure enough, when I asked friends to share their experiences about moving to Fairhope, one woman, who for obvious reasons wants to remain anonymous, shared this story:

"My first lesson after moving to Fairhope was not to show up to a covered-dish luncheon with anything in a plastic bowl. I thought I'd be practical by reusing a big plastic Cammie's Old Dutch Ice Cream tub; it had a handle and everything. The luncheon was at my neighbor's beautiful home. The hostess greeted me with a big smile, took my pasta salad, and kept chatting as she ushered me into the kitchen and, in one seemingly fluid motion, transferred my food into a beautiful glass bowl. She said it looked delicious and was so kind that I didn't get offended at all. I was actually relieved when she put it on the table with all the other pretty bowls and platters. Her table looked like something out of a magazine."

And that story, my friends, is not only a lesson about the importance of using the correct food container for each situation, but also about how to be a gracious hostess.

My family lived in downtown Mobile, but my father and I would visit Fairhope when the downtown roads here were still dirt. I'd walk around Fairhope barefoot, because that's what everyone did then. Daddy told my mother he wanted to purchase a place in Fairhope, and she sniffed her nose in the air and said, "No. I don't like camping."

— **Jule Moon**, born in 1919, graduated in 1936 from Murphy High School in Mobile. After graduating from The University of Texas and living in various places, she finally settled in Fairhope, where she continues to live today at 105 years old.

14

For Everything There Is a Season

Carousel horses move in a flat, repetitive pattern, while a roller coaster takes you on a wild ride of soaring highs and plunging lows. On the ride home, everyone talks about the roller coaster, not the carousel. We remember the ride that made our hearts race.

The plunging lows in life balance our joyful days and keep things in perspective. We work to keep our city lovely because our beautiful environment balances the times we can't see through the dark clouds or flooding tears.

It must be difficult to be overwrought by heartache while living in a gloomy place.

Magazine articles only show the photogenic side of Fairhope, but the truth is, we're a real city with real people who get sick, suffer business losses, and gather to mourn the loss of sweet children. Marriages, friendships, and churches split, while hurricanes literally split houses. The beautiful little town that tourists love to visit and articles claim is perfect is, sadly, all too real.

Friends we've lost come to mind while passing their former houses or seeing their artwork hanging in a downtown office. I never sip a Fairhope Float without imagining our late friend, 94-year-old Virgil Spivey, sitting in the corner of Mr. Gene's Beans with a cup of coffee, greeting the schoolchildren who stopped to get an ice cream cone on their way home.

Sometimes, when I'm sitting at a particular traffic light downtown, I still recall waiting there, on the side of the road, for over 20 minutes while the long funeral procession of a popular high school baseball player passed by. I'd only lived here for two years, and it was the first time I'd witnessed the overwhelming enormity of Fairhope's beautiful compassion. I found myself wiping away tears, even though I didn't know him.

The hospital parking lot has been full of friends waving signs and flashing their car lights to signal their love to a sick friend inside. I've watched as an entire congregation openly wept while baptizing a beautiful smiling infant who was receiving hospice care. Good people deliver food, and strangers show up to pray while you cry. Bouquets of flowers appear on doorsteps, and money is sent anonymously to those in need.

I've never seen a town more compassionate than Fairhope. For now, it's still small enough for people to connect in difficult times, so of course, one of our fears related to growth is the potential loss of connection. Is it possible to live in a large city and still feel a strong link to your neighbors?

When someone you barely know passes you in the grocery store and reaches over to squeeze your hand and say, "Hey, honey, I'm praying for you," you know you're in a good place. But lately, there are more faces in the store that we don't recognize. How will we make this work?

The love felt during the dark times makes the sunsets, parades, and flowers even more vibrant and breathtaking. We appreciate the good because we've lived through the bad. Fairhope is a wild roller coaster–ride kind of town, experiencing beautiful highs and earthly lows, not some magazine's predictable pretty little carousel of a town.

Sometimes, home is where the broken heart is. But the beat goes on.

The Knights of Ecor Rouge toss beads during their Mardi Gras parade.

15

A Small Spiffy Southern Town

Some expect small Southern towns to be full of people in overalls, dirty T-shirts, and bare feet, and although you can always find a bit of that stereotype somewhere, Southerners also have the reputation of being pretty cute.

In Fairhope, you'll see a little bit of everything, from funky to retro to slouchy, with a healthy dose of "lovely." Pretty dresses and sports coats are displayed in store windows and elegantly worn by ladies and gentlemen throughout town.

Some tourists wear coordinated "resort wear casual," which is hard to describe, yet can be spotted a mile away. Standing beneath the town clock while looking bewildered and holding a map doesn't tip us off to the visitor status as much as the togs. Those who have just spent 10 hours in monogrammed minivans with their children spill out onto the sidewalk in wrinkled T-shirts and shorts in search of a shrimp po'boy with a cold Chardonnay for mom. "You kids are on my last nerve," says the mother whose shirt says, "I've got 99 problems, but the beach ain't one."

A good number of Fairhope ladies don't really wear "clothes" but instead wear "outfits." Those who gather for club meetings or lunch aren't overly fancy, but don't bop about in stretchy workout clothes, unless, of course, they are genuinely bopping or working out. The reminder taped to their dressing table mirror is the adage, "Two things don't lie: children and leggings."

The men usually look nice and in the fall wear brightly colored checked shirts in team colors. It's a step above a T-shirt and usually signals they probably attended the school.

Even the slouchy mismatched younger crowd takes great care in obtaining that wild look. We secretly think they're adorable but act aghast so they'll feel bold. Today's hipster is tomorrow's city council member, so we want to encourage their independent spirit. The little girls have hair bows for every occasion, and if they look a mess, we say, "Bless her heart, her daddy must have dressed her."

There's a small crowd that revels in the convenience of fanny packs, comfy shoes, and hiking sticks. They're often heard saying things like, "I just made a set of wind chimes in the shape of a cat."

Last summer, temperatures climbed to a scorching 100 degrees, so my friend Ann and I showed up for coffee at Provision wearing cool, breezy sundresses. At a nearby table, another friend sat with a group of young mothers dressed for tennis in short, flippy skirts, coordinating tops, and hair bows. One, who had obviously given up on life, wore a baseball cap. Their watch bands matched their skirts, and their choice of lipstick was spot-on. "It's so hot; I can't believe y'all've (all of you have) been playing tennis," I commented. "Oh, we haven't," she told me. "We're just in our 'running around' outfits." "Pretend tennis" is obviously a new category of the well-dressed summer lady's closet. Since it's the effort of looking polished that counts, how can you not love them?

Some Fairhopers even show up in public from time to time in creative ensembles that make them look like an elf, Mary Poppins, a Jedi, or The Grinch, for no particular reason other than we sometimes leak creativity and joy all over the place. Moses was spotted walking down the street after Vacation Bible School one day. We recognized him by the top-ten list he carried.

I visited a friend's first-grade class dressed in a Pilgrim costume. In my best British-Southern accent, I asked the children for advice, since my ship had taken a wrong turn and ended up in Mobile Bay. Then, I read them a Thanksgiving story. Afterwards, I just kept the costume on and went to lunch with friends downtown. Why not? People are kind of used to this sort of thing, so no one really cared, and since the friends I met were former teachers, they didn't bat an eye.

The Pilgrim outfit was again pulled from my closet when I needed to get my son's attention after he disrupted his English class at Fairhope Middle School. The same school that was whimsical enough to field a unicycle team a few years before somehow didn't see the humor in an adolescent Jim Gaffigan competing with the teacher for control of the class. The teacher alerted me by email, and like a Mayflower superhero, I threw on my costume and drove like a bat out of Plymouth to the school. This was not his first offense, and he had been warned I was ready and willing to get his attention one way or the other.

I positioned myself directly in front of the doors by the flagpole, garbed in the long black skirt, white pointy collar, and crisp apron, my head covered by the prim and proper white coif. Standing and stewing with my hands on my hips, I waited for the bell to ring, at which time the students burst out of the building, then in unison, screeched to a halt — stunned, still as statues. His eyes met mine, and he slowly looked me up and down with a wave of horror spreading across his face.

A Small Spiffy Southern Town

"Your father and I warned you that if you didn't pay attention to your teacher and our rules, we'd get your attention somehow," I told him. With a breathless pulse of nausea in his voice, he said, "You're ruining my life!"

Mothers in the carpool line blew their horns and waved, knowing exactly what I was doing, as I took him by the arm (partly to keep him from fainting) and escorted him to the car. Several mothers sent text messages asking to borrow the costume. The principal sent me a note that said we were "sisters from other mothers" because while raising her two boys, she once showed up at their cafeteria dressed as Aretha Franklin with a big wig and sparkly dress and sang, "R-E-S-P-E-C-T" — and believe me, she earned it that day.

There's no need for expensive clothing in Fairhope. The General Meeting of the Committee for the Preservation of Loveliness welcomes women wearing both high-priced designer and bargain-shop styles. Effort always wins over price.

Because we're close to the Gulf of Mexico, some transplants think they are recreating a scene from *Hawaii Five-O* and wear flip-flops and Hawaiian shirts 365 days a year so they can write about it in their Christmas letters to send "back home." Fairhopers don't really consider this to be a beach town. That distinction goes to the spectacular nearby towns of Gulf Shores and Orange Beach. The Nix Center newsletter published an announcement that, in a softened, Southern, round-about way, said, "Unless you are a surfer, or professional sandcastle architect, there's no need to expose your gnarly octogenarian toes every single cotton-picking day." The card-playing seniors grumbled but got the message.

Another piece of valuable advice is don't show up at Julwin's at 10:30 in the morning wearing all black unless you want everyone to put their coffee down and give you the "pouty sad face." It's their way of saying, "I'm sorry for your loss."

Someone will surely come right out and ask, "Who died?" because we're curious and hate to miss a good funeral luncheon. Deviled eggs taste better with a drizzling of salty tears.

Fairhope is still just enough old-time Southern to adhere to many of the standard rules and rituals our grandparents taught. And it's not just the older crowd. Many younger folks were also raised to know things like, "Never wear white shoes before Easter or after Labor Day." There should be no arguments about this, no quoting a 20-year-old self-proclaimed "influencer" who writes for a publication that has "Southern" in the title but hires writers from Seattle who also thinks skipping thank-you notes and serving gray gelatinous stuffing rather than cornbread dressing is OK.

The white shoes rule boils down to this: since the South can be as hot as new love 12 months a year, white shoes let us know where we are on the calendar. They are a marker. When the weather is crazy, we depend upon the language of clothing to set us straight.

A 75-degree day can show up at any time of the year, but 75 degrees and brown suede boots signal we're close to Thanksgiving. Seventy-five degrees and white sandals say, "I hope you had a lovely Easter," and a 75-degree day with a plaid wool skirt is the signal to shout, "Let's go caroling!" The weather may try to trick us, but our wardrobe keeps us straight. It's all about clarity and order.

Try walking up to someone on October 17th, giving them a pinch, and saying, "Ha, ha, ha! You aren't wearing green," and see how that goes.

The exception to the white shoes rule is that brides, babies, and majorettes are allowed to wear white shoes or boots all year. Because who doesn't absolutely adore brides, babies, and majorettes? I'm pretty sure it's been an official amendment to the Alabama state constitution since 1887.

There's an effervescent group of ladies running around Fairhope in December who sport matching Santa dresses with white boots. They limit it to one night each year, and because I adore 98% of them, we'll go ahead and make an exception. It's a Fairhope sort of thing, so they're excused for this one night as charming and jolly little rebels.

Crazed football fans wear T-shirts that say, "We're gonna whoop ya," and the teenager bagging groceries sometimes wears the big pig costume. Artists walk around in paint-splattered smocks, and farmers wear overalls. After a pastor's untucked shirt flew up when he raised his arms in praise and worship, there was a terrifying moment of spotlighted hairy belly, which led me to knock back an entire box of Altoids to counteract the gag reflex in my throat. It was then I decided that pastors absolutely need a suit, or at least a tucked-in shirt with belt, or better yet, a long black robe. See? There's a reason for the uniforms in society. Would you be comfortable if your doctor showed up for your exam dressed in a Burger King uniform?

I instinctively flinched and reached for my phone to summon the police one morning as I dropped my son off in the school carpool line and witnessed a scruffy man in wrinkled cargo shorts, dirty T-shirt, and flip-flops approaching the young children as they exited the cars. After a quick mom-squeal, "Agh!" my son said, "Mom, it's OK, that's Mr. Whifflebom, one of our teachers." The highly qualified yet clueless man's unfortunate choice of apparel almost landed him in the fashion jail, reinforcing the need for societal fashion rules.

The Grand Summer Ball is Fairhope's most elegant night of the year, benefiting Thomas Hospital, with ladies in flowing, colorful gowns and men sporting summery white dinner jackets. It's rivaled only by some extravagant kiddie birthday parties, but come now, you only turn two once. Why not go all-out?

A Small Spiffy Southern Town

Fairhope fashion spans all occasions with a time, rhyme, and reason for everything. You'll find shorts and T-shirts at pre-dawn Jubilees, where scooping up fish and crabs calls for quick comfort, and you'll see plenty of boots at a barn dance. I once saw a lovely couple dressed in exquisite formalwear at Judge Roy Bean's as a goat casually walked through the room. There's a time for gilded masks, a time for spray-painted Nikes with beverages dipped from a lined garbage can, and a time for seersucker, bowties, and champagne in crystal. Knowing the appropriate dress code for each occasion is a valuable lifetime skill.

Men wear hats; gentlemen remove them indoors. And if they wear their hat inside my house, it's a sure bet, like sorority rush, they will be on the N.I.B. list - not invited back. May Moss has the spiritual gift of sweeping past a man, extending her hand, and saying matter of factly, "Here, honey, I'll take that hat for you." She said she's never had anyone refuse to hand over their dirty old baseball cap. "I'll put it right here next to the front door so you won't forget it," she concludes with a smile that could charm the devil – whose horns are most certainly attached to a baseball cap he wears indoors.

However we dress, we do it with careful consideration. Styles may come and go, but demonstrating a bit of effort is the same as showing respect, and respect for one another is always in style.

We are only 45 minutes apart, but in Orange Beach, "casual" is a T-shirt. In Fairhope, that's a blazer!
—**Andy Andrews**, New York Times bestselling author and Baldwin County resident

16

Don't Throw That Jar Away

Little did Leslie Presson know, her cheerful new home in Fairhope would one day become a place of darkness, but from that time of sadness, a new ministry of hope would bloom — quite literally.

Having relocated from Memphis seven years earlier with her husband's career change, Leslie's world jerked to a halt with a diagnosis of aggressive breast cancer. In the agonizing months that followed, she faced the difficult journey so many others have traveled and battled the sickness, fear, and pain of harsh treatments. Leslie prayed not only that God would heal her so she could spend many more years with her family but also that something good would come from her illness. In time, God answered her prayers with healing and a surprising path that would bring joy to the entire town.

Friends, neighbors, and church members all reached out to Leslie during her cancer treatments. Some sent cards, others delivered food, but almost everyone brought flowers. Fairhope is full of gardeners, and yards overflow with colorful blooms that are the perfect way to cheer a sick friend. Leslie's kitchen and living room were in a constant state of floral overload. She said, "The flowers were a beautiful reminder that someone cared about me. They reflected the beauty of God's world, and I studied the small details of each one.

"My daughter was married a few years before I was sick, and the flowers I was receiving kept reminding me of her wedding arrangements and how I thought it was such a shame to toss them all out at the end of the day. It bothered me no one got to take her wedding flowers home to enjoy," she recalls.

Leslie was struck with an idea in the most marvelous way possible — while dreaming. While she slept, a new idea formed, along with a complete operational plan and even a logo. So convinced this was meant to be, Leslie put her plan into action. Soon, she and her friend Dorothy Lagarde gathered eight friends to help brainstorm, and Hope Blooms was launched.

Basically a floral recycling operation, Hope Blooms gathers expensive floral arrangements and doubles their lifespan in order to spread happiness and beauty to many others. Now a regular part of party planning in

Fairhope, the florists and wedding planners know to inform their clients of the opportunity to donate to Hope Blooms.

Hope Blooms organizes late-night "pick-up teams," who arrive at party and reception venues all over Fairhope after partygoers and dancers have drifted home for the evening. As tables are removed and floors swept in the wee hours of the night, the team takes leftover flowers, which include everything from small tabletop arrangements to massive archway stunners. Flowers have even been donated from Mardi Gras balls, funerals, and corporate events.

The aromatic deliveries are transported to the Hope Blooms warehouse, originally located in Leslie's home kitchen. Bright and early Monday morning, another team arrives and disassembles the large arrangements. They trim and organize the flowers and greenery to create many smaller arrangements. The perky nosegays and bouquets are placed in plain jars repurposed into vases donated by seemingly everyone in town.

"Don't throw that jar away!" has become the standard order in kitchens all over Fairhope: Jars that held Wickles Pickles, applesauce, and gravy are all washed and saved to be filled with flowers. "Well, I swanee! I never knew you could buy gravy in a jar!" cried all the hard-core Southern cooks in town.

"Store-bought gravy?"

"Yes, the Yankees created a demand for it."

"No, they claim not to like gravy."

"Their gravy is tomato sauce."

"That's just weird."

"Gravy in a jar. My grandmother would just die all over again."

Remaining fresh — as a daisy — the flowers are then delivered by yet another team to anyone who could use some cheer. Nursing homes, new neighbors, police officers, teachers, hospital staff members, and yes, those battling cancer. Recipients are surprised and feel loved when someone stops by to bring them flowers.

"It's so much more than flowers," Leslie said. "People from all over town are volunteering and making new friends because of the connection Hope Blooms provides." Yes, the recipients are always cheered and encouraged by the gift, but those doing the work and making the deliveries feel the love reflected to them tenfold.

Family members and friends who were overwrought with worry while they sat in the hospital waiting room on Christmas Eve were at first confused when offered flowers. "How much are you charging?" they asked.

"Nothing," Leslie and her delivery team replied. "They're just to let you know that someone is thinking about you during the holidays." Within a few minutes, everyone in the waiting room was holding a beautiful floral arrangement, and most had tears in their eyes like it was the best Christmas present they'd ever received. Leslie said, "They just needed a little bit of hope."

A few couples who had smaller weddings that didn't require a professional wedding planner were so excited about the concept of sharing their flowers that they made their own plans to donate to Hope Blooms. One couple went so far as to load their own truck with flowers and, on their way to their New Orleans honeymoon, drove to Leslie's house and tooted the horn. "Hey! We brought these for you to use," they shouted, and giggled and waved as they drove away with paper streamers flying from the tailgate.

Donations and annual fundraising events cover workspace rent, informational materials, worktables, utilities, and other incidentals.

Light overcomes darkness, and the beauty of flowers overcomes a long list of ailments. Leslie Presson is now cancer-free, and her dream of sharing beauty has touched not only the recipients of bouquets but has also softened the hearts of brides, florists, late-night pick-up team members, flower arrangers, the delivery squad, and the all-important gravy jar savers.

It's yet another way Fairhopers and flowers connect with other people and keep our city beautiful.

17

An Afternoon at the Ballet

Amid the chaotic whirlwind of Christmastime rush and the ever-changing landscape of our town, I was feeling a bit frazzled. Nothing seemed right that year. Feeling out of sorts, I took my mother to a matinee performance of *The Nutcracker* at the Fairhope Civic Center because I had promised a teenage friend I would attend her show.

The curtain opened and children dressed in beautiful costumes danced across the stage — the same stage where my son had his "walk out" for senior prom and where I've watched plays and listened to cantankerous political forums.

The Snow Queen, once a timid child I remembered hiding behind her father at the Arts and Crafts Festival, now commanded the stage with grace and confidence. Her metamorphosis from shy little girl to engaging performer seemed to happen overnight, but had it really been five, no, ten years ago when I first met her? A few of the tiny mice scampering across the stage were in Vacation Bible School with me that past summer, and one of the Chinese Tea dancers had sung Christmas hymns next to me earlier that morning. It all started to feel very familiar, like family.

At intermission, we enjoyed the concession area with homemade cookies, baked by the dancers' mothers and wrapped in cellophane bags with curled ribbons. I introduced my mom to friends and neighbors I'd known for years. The lights had to be flashed multiple times to break up the mini-reunions and bring us back to our seats.

As a fan of the ballerina who portrayed Clara, I saved my most enthusiastic round of applause for her. I know and love four generations of her family, and this responsible teen also feeds my dog when I'm out of town. I felt so proud of her as she danced her role perfectly.

Actually, all of the lead roles were danced with elegance and precision, while the younger parts were performed with off-the-chart cuteness, but the thing that shone brightest was the spirit of Fairhope that I found onstage and in the audience. A small-town ballet company wasn't being featured as much as the community itself.

An Afternoon at the Ballet

While little ballerinas grow up and move away to college and life beyond Fairhope, the memories they've left behind will tie them to their hometown forever, and us, to them.

As the final curtain fell and we walked to the exit, a familiar voice called out my name. Turning, I was met with the embrace of Gianna, my favorite ballerina, who had brought Clara to life onstage. "I was hoping you'd be here, thank you for coming!" In that moment, I realized that despite the hectic holiday and the inevitability of change, the heart of our small town remained steadfast. Sometimes it takes an afternoon at the ballet to figure that out.

"Used to be" (or years ago) when I met someone new, I would ask, "Who are your people?" Nowadays I ask, "Where are you from?" If they say, "Well, I'm a Yankee," I answer, "That's ok. You're only a Damn Yankee if you tell us the way they do things up North is better."
— **Harriet Outlaw**, "Used to be" teacher and still storyteller, local folklore lover

18

It's Just "Stuff"

Discussing the camaraderie and neighborliness that emerge during and after a hurricane can be irresponsible, because we've also learned that storms can tear our hearts out with death and catastrophic destruction. It's a danger of living here that we take seriously, yet at the same time, we don't get too worked up over the smaller storms. Newcomers amuse us when they run around boarding up houses when a small tropical storm approaches. Claudia said, "The same people who won't touch gluten or dairy are miraculously healed when a hurricane comes and they grab all the bread and milk in town." Then again, we've seen small storms morph into major atmospheric events overnight, so there's always an edge of uneasiness during hurricane season.

MaryLou had severe damage to her kitchen area during the last hurricane. She's the third generation to live in her family's bay house, constructed of local pine and originally built by her grandfather. Over the years, the house grew into a meandering floor plan with several porches overlooking Mobile Bay. MaryLou had just remodeled the upstairs sleeping porch so her grandchildren, still babies now, could someday "fall asleep to the sound of lapping waves beneath the glow of the moon." Described by friends as a "traditional sandy-floored mansion," her house was one of the most charming, well-loved homes in town.

The slow-moving hurricane hurled a tree limb through the kitchen window, which allowed a deluge of water and wind damage.

MaryLou wore a Bill-E's T-shirt and running shorts, along with her pearls — because coastal chicks of all ages know the first thing you do when there's a sign of a tropical disturbance is to pop the pearls on, ensuring we're prepared for anything. Our beloved jewels from the sea, reminiscent of creamy grits and white magnolias, won't be misplaced in the chaos. If the worst happens and we're carried off to the funeral home, we'll be appropriately adorned for the viewing.

Stepping carefully through the mess, MaryLou saw the lower kitchen cabinets were cracked and dripping wet. Kicking muck out of the way, she held her breath and reached into the water-soaked cabinet to feel for her

It's Just "Stuff"

grandmother's deep 13″ cast-iron skillet. "I just seasoned that pan two weeks ago," she sniffed. "It's my favorite."

The only thing a storm organizes is a list of things we hold dear. Nature swirls everything into a neatly arranged hierarchy. At the top of our list are our people. We make sure everyone we love is safe. Next come the pets, neighbors, the family Bible, photo albums, great-grandpa's violin that sat on the bookshelf, and the box of love notes that Hallmark could never replicate. We take inventory of the most valuable things with a lump in our throats.

MaryLou had far pricier things in her home than an old cast-iron skillet, yet upon seeing the smashed window and room full of leaves and water, it was the only thing in her kitchen she wanted.

Some things can be replaced; others can't, and it breaks our hearts. We tell ourselves they're just "things — stuff — objects," but sometimes those things represent our loves, stories, hopes, and dreams, and it hurts to see them blown away.

It may look like a little piece of paper dancing in the wind or a plastic toy washing down the street, but to us, it's our story. It's the last note our mother ever wrote to us on the back of an Annie Armstrong Easter envelope or the Happy Meal toy our son instructed us to keep in our pocket on his first day of school so we wouldn't be lonely.

Hurricanes make us think material things shouldn't matter, yet we know they do.

MaryLou wiped the drywall jibbles from her skillet with the tail of her shirt, and after dragging the limbs off the outdoor grill, slid the skillet over hot coals and began cooking up every bit of shrimp in her thawing freezer before it spoiled. She fed the people she loved, just as her mother and grandmother had done in the aftermath of hurricanes long ago. Her people gathered 'round, safe, exhausted, but well fed.

Some of MaryLou's "stuff" was ruined, but her stories were intact. It wasn't just an old skillet. To her, it was a salvaged treasure that connected generations of strong Gulf Coast women who somehow managed to survive the storms of life.

19

Would You Live in an Agrihood?

Although most of us don't own a tractor, and few even know the names of the crops being grown other than the iconic corn or cotton, we somehow feel connected with the local farms, so it saddens us to see them plowed up and planted with "progress."

Like the rest of the United States, farms in Fairhope are being sold to make way for shopping malls, subdivisions, schools, and skating rinks. It's the great paving of America, and there's not much we can do about it.

Or is there?

A new trend in neighborhood construction may seem odd, but it has enough merit to consider. "Agrihoods" may be the answer we've been looking for to bridge our housing expansion and our desire to keep our rural connection. The innovative agrihood neighborhood concept replaces the traditional golf course with a small working farm as the center of community activity.

Homeowner dues go towards the hired farm manager, not a groundskeeper or golf pro. Residents are invited to regular gatherings to learn more about the planting schedule and receive encouragement for their backyard gardens. Pesticides for manicured greens are traded for friendly ducks that eat insects and other old methods to stimulate crop production. The golf carts are replaced by tractors, wagons, and wheelbarrows.

Children watch out their windows while peanuts are harvested, and everyone gathers on a Saturday morning to pick fresh blueberries or satsumas from the orchard.

Markets are held throughout the year to sell produce that helps fund farm activities. After residents have shopped, the market is open to the public, who will undoubtedly comment on how they wish they lived in this pocket of Eden.

Agrihoods could help small towns maintain their farming legacy while providing new housing options. Other agrihoods are springing up across the country, allowing families to learn how fresh vegetables are grown and feel like they are part of the all-American dream.

With over 100 agrihoods currently operating nationwide, perhaps it's time local developers examine this alternative to traditional neighborhoods. Sure, it will be a bumpy process to try something new, but the founders of Fairhope embraced bold ideas, and agrihoods may fit right into the creative Fairhope spirit of innovative adventure.

Imagine children in the agrihood ignoring their phones and video games to discuss instead the problems of pecan phylloxera or debating the age-old question, "Are Better Boy tomatoes really better? — than what?"

Sheep may safely graze in a pasture where neighbors meet one another on their evening walks, stopping to admire the new calf born last week. The idea of rocking on the community barn porch with neighbors while watching your corn pop up in rows could be just the answer we've been looking for.

It's (fresh) food for thought.

Fairhope Yacht Club, as seen from the mouth of Fly Creek.

20

Overheard in Latte Da

I'm fixin' to tell you the God's honest truth
So quit actin' ugly and bein' aloof

Sweeter than honey, my grandbaby girl
Pretty as punch, oh joy to the world

Was your mama a Kappa? Oh girlfriend,
no way
She went Tri Delta and loved it back in her day

The Yacht Club is hosting a holiday dinner
I haven't been there in months, but Daddy's a member

Leslie Anne Tarabella

That man in the corner? He's so very nice
His brother, my broker, gave good advice

Although good grief, his wife's a hot mess
With stories that stir up a big hornet's nest

Your headband's so cute with that monogram
I'll swing by The Pig to pick up the ham

Baste it with Co-Cola and pineapple juice
Cover with foil but keep it real loose

Her mama raised her right, but I fear
she used paper plates on Easter Sunday, my dear

But she'll make it up at Christmas, you know
With her holiday china stealing the show

This ice cream's supposed to be sugar free
But I think it's loaded with big calories

You've given my day a very a good start
Call me real soon and bless your
Pea-pickin' heart

21

Hop on the Walking School Bus

It really isn't all that far, but when you have little-bitty legs, walking to school seems like a grand adventure.

When schools were removed from viable neighborhood locations and relocated into sprawling, soulless buildings on the outskirts of town — well, you see where I'm going with this. I don't think I'm the only one troubled by the trend, as we now face morning gridlock with waves of cars and buses transporting sleepy children to school.

If you add the congested streets to a swirl of societal woes and parental fears, the all-American act of walking to school disappears. And did someone whisper, "Childhood obesity"? Could it all be related?

Perhaps it's due to all the good coffee shops around town, but our Fairhope minds don't stay idle very long. Bing-bing-bing — we're thinkers. And community leader Charlene Lee had a bright idea. Developing a plan that would encourage children to safely walk to school in a protected and chaperoned group at least once a week, she got busy and made it happen.

"It's a walking school bus!" sang the children of Fairhope.

Dropped off at strategic points, about a half mile or a bit more from their school, children are checked in, warmed up, and encouraged to do their best. Carrying their backpacks, they skip, twirl, sing, and even lollygag on occasion to make it up the hill to school. A few adults walk along and serve as crossing guards and cheerleaders.

Community volunteers have also shown up to have "chance encounters" with the students and mysteriously emerge from behind a tree or from our local Mosher Castle dressed like a princess or troll. Shrek even made an appearance, and Santa Claus has been known to join the Walking School Bus when he's in town, making his list and checking it twice. There's always something amazing to see along the route. Whether it's new flowers being planted on the corners, seasonal decorations in people's yards, new businesses opening, or even fairies dancing in a field, it's all wonderful and entirely true. Ask the children.

Our tots are valued, as are our seniors and all those in between. When we have gifts to share, like Charlene's experience in fitness and community resources, or her other volunteers who serve with the schools or the Baldwin County Trailblazers, everything comes together in a connection that produces magical experiences, not to mention good health and shorter carpool lines.

I just wonder how many sessions I would have needed with the school guidance counselor if a troll had popped out from behind a tree to say "good morning" to me as a second grader. I was more of a Mary Poppins sing-along kind of girl.

Still, connections are important for everyone, and making contact with our youngest residents ensures no one is left out of the Fairhope fun.

*New people are moving here so fast,
I don't have time to piss them all off anymore.*
— **Mike Lyons**, owner of Lyons Share Custom Framing and Gallery

22

Two New Activities

Bird-watching, doll collecting, cooking, and playing the harmonica are just a few of the activities of groups you can belong to in Fairhope, but lately, two particular groups stand out from the rest: one for being so large, and the other for appearing on the scene, seemingly overnight, and taking the town by storm.

According to my calculations, approximately 1,500 to 2,500 people in Fairhope now participate in weekly Bible studies. Due to the population increase, or perhaps because of the sinning nature of the world, the number of small groups has grown wildly in the last decade.

Bible studies aren't unique to Fairhope alone but are prevalent, especially throughout the South and many other regions. The question, "Which Bible study are you taking this year?" is as common and non-offensive as if someone asked, "Where do you get your oil changed?"

There are two large local groups, each with over 300 participants, while smaller groups gather in churches, homes, and coffee shops, sometimes from a blend of denominational backgrounds, for in-depth study of the Bible. I sat in on Rabbi Steven Silberman's Women of the Old Testament class when he visited from Ahavas Chesed Synagogue in Mobile. There's something for everyone, and I've never heard of any group that wouldn't welcome someone new, even if they have doubts or questions. While some studies are profoundly theological and dissect word origins and trace lineages, others give a more basic overview.

Those participating in the studies will be the first to admit they're sinful humans and flawed piles of D-I-R-T. The highest church attendance usually occurs right after Mardi Gras. When we're reminded to "kill them with kindness," our minds often jump to where we'll hide the body. We are all prone to be jealous hypocrites, cheaters, thieves, and some have even been brazen enough to try and pass off store-bought cake as their own. It's the forgiveness part we cherish.

The danger is that sitting in the cool church basement sipping coffee and discussing Zechariah is much easier than actually getting out and visiting a

Two New Activities

nursing home or painting a family's porch. Balance and joy are found when we put what we learn into action and don't think that the studies and perfect attendance pin are the actual stairway to heaven. (But the pin does look pretty when it sparkles in the sunlight.) It goes without saying that if you volunteer to work in Vacation Bible School, you're on the fast track to sainthood.

When thousands of imperfect hurting people are trying to improve, it's a good thing. Maybe that's another reason Fairhope is full of kindness. We're a work in progress. (But it's not all about works — just thought I'd toss that in for, well, you know who you are.)

The second trending group in town are the pickleballers. Pickleball is a game that has suddenly grown into such a big deal that the City of Fairhope installed new pickleball courts in two different locations and more are said to be on the way. I don't know how many people participate, but almost everyone I know is talking about it. I loved the racquetball craze in the '80s, but that came and went. Pickleball will surely last forever, right? There's a line waiting to play almost every day, even during the hottest months. Some church gymnasiums around town have opened their air-conditioned gyms for pickleball, combining the new game with yet another opportunity for even more Bible study.

I don't understand the game because I've never played, but I hear it's like a miniature tennis match without all the pesky running. You can have designer paddles, which intrigues me, and there are also cute outfits involved. I am trying to figure out why I have yet to try this fun game. Maybe I've been too busy studying the Bible.

Ever since The Kickball Incident in fourth grade, I've not been a fan of competition that doesn't involve a crown. After a heated kickball tournament on a dusty playground, which I cared nothing about because it interrupted my clover-chain weaving, a boy from the other team almost crashed into me, kicking up a cloud of dust. Nose to nose, his stinky sweat splashed onto my arm, and his red face scrunched up as he screamed, "We beat you! We beat you!" It was totally horrifying. I was very timid in those days, so I remained silent, yet thought to myself, "But it didn't get you into the Red Bird reading group, did it?" Then I cried and hated sports forever.

That's why I don't know much about pickleball. All that competition is stressful, and I'd hate to deal with a screaming bad sport. I'd have to ask my Bible study group to pray for him.

23

Santa Knows She Pushed

For the last decade or so, I've been the on-air host for WABF radio station's live broadcast of the Fairhope Magical Christmas Parade. WABF on-air personality Mark Swally and I describe the details of the parade for those who can't attend in person while the station manager, Lori DuBose, rides in the parade to the cheers of her loyal listeners. Tuning in on their radios or through the internet, listeners can hear the description of their hometown parade while stationed overseas, away at college, or just around the corner.

After the high school band and majorettes have marched by, the main event finally appears. The Jolly Old Elf himself rolls down the street, high atop the Fairhope Volunteer Fire Department hook and ladder truck. Giant reindeer cutouts line the sides of the truck as helper elves toss candy to the crowd. Both old and young are awestruck at the beauty and sweetness of the sight. Some children shout and wave, while others stand in stunned silence, and a few in repentant fear. One year, my five-year-old saw Santa wave in his direction and breathlessly said, "Santa 'rememborized' me."

I wouldn't say I'm his number-one favorite, but I've heard Santa is grateful to know his elves back at the North Pole can tune in to our internet broadcast. They reportedly cheer and toss marshmallows every time I say the word "sparkly."

It's through this connection that Santa agreed to give me an exclusive interview. His close friend, Cecil Christenberry, set up the meeting on a discreet park bench overlooking Mobile Bay. We had to keep a low profile to avoid a mob scene.

I started by asking, "Santa, since you can go anywhere in the world, why do you choose to visit Fairhope, Alabama, every year just before Christmas?"

Santa almost blew his cover by loudly laughing, "Fair-ho-ho-hope!" He chuckled at his clever joke, then went on, "Well, Mrs. Claus and I like to catch our breath before the big rush, and Fairhope is the perfect place to do that. Mrs. Claus visits the children in Fairhope in November for the

Santa Knows She Pushed

Lighting of the Trees, then I visit a few weeks later in December for the Christmas parade."

Santa thought for a moment, then said, "Even though the parade is exciting, I think the real magic in Fairhope begins with the Lighting of the Trees just before Thanksgiving, and Mrs. Claus always gives me a full report from the children she sees that night. You aren't going to believe this, but the glow from your downtown lights can sometimes be seen at the North Pole!

"The elves claimed they could even hear the crowd counting down. Come to think of it, last year's celebration was when my friend Charlene Lee was asked to pull the light switch. It's a big honor, you know. I always get to see Charlene when she invites me to join her and the children on the Walking School Bus. It's one of my favorite things to do while I'm in town."

I couldn't stand it, so I had to ask, "Santa, did Mrs. Claus tell you that a woman tried to push people in the crowd at the Tree Lighting a few years ago?" Santa looked sad and said, "Don't worry. She learned her lesson." Then, he spoke Southern so I would understand and added, "Bless her heart."

"A lump of coal?" I asked.

"Santa keeps his gift list private," he warned, with a sly smile.

Remembering something, Santa snapped his fingers and said, "I also can't think of all the beautiful twinkling trees downtown without remembering another friend, Joyce Stowe. She was always on my 'nice' list as a little girl and grew up with a love for Fairhope and had the idea for magical twinkling trees. She was so happy years later, to finally see her dream come true. Children who grow up and put their dreams into action like Charlene and Joyce is what makes Fairhope hold a special place in my heart."

With a brightness on his face, he added, "Speaking of dreams coming true, one night, just before I climbed aboard the fire truck to ride in the parade, I stopped to talk with a wide-eyed little girl who was snuggled in the arms of her mother. But then, I looked into their faces and somehow knew they had been on their own for a while (Santa has a way of knowing these things). The beautiful young mother had a sadness about her. I took a deep breath and said, 'You know, Christmas isn't just for children.' The young mother nodded, then I added, 'Why don't you turn around and look behind you?' She was confused at first, so I repeated myself, and she finally turned and saw the man she loved, kneeling on one knee and holding a beautiful engagement ring. The crowd was holding their breath and broke into cheers as a new family formed right before our eyes."

Santa Claus looked out over Mobile Bay and seemed to think aloud. "There are good little children all over the world, but I find that Fairhope children are especially grateful, loving, and respectful. They also have big hearts and, in the true meaning of Christmas, love to give as much as receive. The City of Fairhope should be congratulated for coming together and raising such wonderful children." The man with the white beard looked right into my eyes and added, "It's such an honor to be received so enthusiastically every year. Keep working together to keep the magic alive, and remember, I'm always watching, so be good, for goodness' sake!"

And I kid you not, like dry leaves before the wild hurricane fly, the Jolly Old Elf swirled and suddenly resembled dancing lightning bugs that sparkled and rose over my head into the pines. And I heard him exclaim, as he flew over the bay, "Merry Christmas, Fair-ho-ho-hope, I'll love you always!"

Even though the city pier has been rebuilt with sturdy concrete, we still think about the afternoons in the '60s when our Dad would take us fishing after he worked all day at his Fram's Southside Market. In those days, it was a rickety wooden pier, and we'd have to be careful that our legs didn't slip through the rough deckboards. We loved time with Dad and catching fish and crabs.
— **Sisters Sharon Fram Davis and Leslie Fram West**, co-owners of 4 Bags Boutique.

24

The Dog Days in Fairhope

The social media post said, "We just moved to Fairhope from California, and the movers left the gate open, and our cocker spaniel escaped." They posted a photo and added, "If you see her, please let us know. She answers to the name of Tiki."

The responses startled them. "I'll watch out for her when I'm over that way," said one man. "Hope you find Tiki soon. She's a cutie," said another. "I think I saw her around dinner time near Uncle Sam's gas station." Others added, "Welcome to town; we're praying you find your little dog."

"Back in California, people would have cursed and shamed us," the surprised dog owner told me.

"Why in the world would they do that?" I didn't understand.

"They would have wanted to scold us for being careless," the husband said.

"But it wasn't your fault. An open gate is what dogs live for."

"Yeah, but some people don't see it that way," they said, shrugging their shoulders.

Fluffy little Tiki was found, and the person who delivered her back to her home became the couple's new friend.

They were beginning to understand Fairhope's kindness and love of dogs.

My own vizsla mix, Doug, a rescue who had been abused as a young pup, ran away from his captor in a dramatic escape (or so he said). After wandering the streets for what appeared to be at least a week, Doug found my husband, who bandaged the dog's bloody feet and pulled the duct tape from his short coat. (See? There are a few mean folks in town.) Doug was a trembling, starving mess of skin and bones and begged us to take him in. How could we say no?

The Dog Days in Fairhope

Doug and I loved taking midday walks around the dog-friendly South Beach Park along the bay. One unbearably hot summer morning, Doug overheard a squirrel, who must have said something very rude about me, and to defend my honor lunged at the twitchy rodent with a plan to kill the son of a gun. In the process, I was dragged to the ground. Four or five people came running to help. Some ran after the dog, while others lifted me to my feet and expressed concern over my bloody knee while helping to pull grass from my teeth.

Grown adults with arms waving and hair flying went running and screaming, "Stop Doug! Doug, come back!" Following the squirrel and dog over the flower beds and around the trees towards the beach, we were only able to grab Doug when he stopped to roll on a dead fish. "Ahh! This hot dead fish feels so good when I smash it into my coat," the hooligan beast said to himself. My car was never the same, and that good-for-nothing squirrel thought he was hilarious. Everyone at the park went home with a good story. And my husband took over dog-walking duties from then on.

Downtown businesses place water bowls on the sidewalks for parched passing pups, with one store posting the sign, "Water for your dog, or short people with low standards, we don't judge."

Our stray dogs and cats can live at The Haven, a no-kill shelter, until someone adopts them, no matter how long it takes. A large group of volunteers fosters, trains, and cares for the animals until they locate a permanent home. Fairhopers drop off old blankets and towels for the cuddling and snuggling process. Everyone pitches in to help.

The primary fundraiser for The Haven is the annual Mystic Mutts of Revelry dog parade, held during Mardi Gras. Wearing clever costumes, pets, along with their humans, parade through the streets of Fairhope behind a police escort. Some mutts with tiny legs ride in wagons or other vehicles decorated to look like fighter jets or farm tractors. Larger dogs trot next to their human on leashes, dressed as clowns, butterflies, or the Tin Man from *The Wizard of Oz*. Dachshunds dressed as hot dogs never get old. My dog, Doug, does not participate since there is a chance that someone could dress their Chihuahua like a squirrel.

Fairhope dogs have the same power to soothe as do the flowers and sunsets. Their eyes look into yours, calming your heart and slowing your breath until you are smitten with their charm.

Yes, this dog loves you.

Or perhaps you smell like a dead fish.

25

Sign of the Times

I've spotted him sitting on the side of the four-lane about three days a week near the Winn Dixie. Appearing to be homeless, he sometimes sleeps in the soft grass shaded by a magnolia tree. It's May, with sweet-smelling flowers and pleasant daytime weather, so he seems comfortable. We're unaccustomed to seeing people sleep on the side of the road in our small town, so many people stop their cars to offer help, but he acts like we're bothering him. Could kindhearted Fairhopers be a bit overwhelming for someone wanting to catch a nap on the side of the road? The word on the street is that the Fairhope police have it all under control and regularly communicate with him to make sure he's okay. Meanwhile, cars continue to stop and offer assistance, and are met with, "I don't need no help," followed with a polite, "but thank ya, anyway."

Visible homelessness wasn't an issue in Fairhope until recently. About a decade ago, a woman began sleeping on the outdoor benches of the library, and the entire town ran to help with offers of hotel rooms, cash, and food. In the end of the years-long saga, the woman turned out to be a colossal scammer who took advantage of the kindhearted people in town — but that's an incredible tale for another day. As a result of her trickery, we're on guard and don't want to be bamboozled again, but this time, it seems to be for real. It's yet another sign of the big world making its way to our small town.

Although the man on Greeno Road can be seen by everyone in town, for years we've had agencies and individuals taking care of those who are struggling yet remain almost invisible to the public.

It's hard to be hurting in a town where everyone appears to be polished and perfect. Thank goodness, we are a close-knit town with those who have the gift of detecting a need before it escalates.

A friend realized one of the families with a child on his son's soccer team was being evicted from their rental house and had nowhere to go. He quickly made a few phone calls to church members and put the family in touch with a wonderful group, Family Promise, who offered them temporary housing and job counseling until they got back on their feet.

Sign of the Times

One of my favorite places to shop has been quietly hiring those in need of work and making sure they have safe living conditions for years.

Deann Servos took a leap of faith and founded Prodisee Pantry in nearby Spanish Fort over 20 years ago to assist with emergency food needs and offer job training programs. It seems like everyone I know has pitched in at some point to help them load and sort food boxes. It's one of the most efficient and successful food distribution operations in our entire region.

Closer to home, several Fairhope churches joined forces over 50 years ago to establish Ecumenical Ministries, which offers all types of aid to community members. In addition to building wheelchair ramps and making structural repairs to homes, they also provide hot meals and clothing for those needing extra care. This centralized ministry streamlines efforts and avoids duplicating programs.

Volunteering a few years ago to interview the applicants for Ecumenical Ministries 'Christmas Sharing toy program, I was brought to tears each time I sat with a parent who told of a sudden job loss, death of a spouse, or debilitating illness of a child that resulted in substantial medical bills. The parents all requested warm coats for their children before they ever asked for a simple doll or bicycle.

Sally Deane, the longtime executive director of Ecumenical Ministries, said Fairhope is the most giving community she's ever known. Time after time, individual donors, churches, and civic groups have come through to see that everyone is cared for.

I suspect the man sleeping beneath the magnolias won't be there long. With temperatures rising and so many viable resources, he's sure to find the help he needs. It's an ever-changing world and yet another reminder that we're no longer a small town. But thank goodness, we're a town that cares.

26

Neighborhood Bridges

"My feet hurt," the eighth-grade girl answered when her teacher asked why she was shuffling. Sure enough, her faded sneakers were tight and in such bad condition they were almost falling apart. Later, the teacher had a quick and quiet word with the school's guidance counselor, and by the next morning, a new pair of sneakers and a pair of slip-on flats had been delivered to the school by an anonymous donor. It was quick, with no committee meeting and no paperwork. It's philanthropy with common sense.

"Here are today's opportunities for kindness..." is how the email begins. Nearly 2,000 Fairhope residents receive this message every morning, alerting them to the needs of children in our community. Does someone need a new school shirt? Does a teenager need toiletries? Don't worry; help is on its way.

Neighborhood Bridges isn't exclusive to Fairhope but is yet another opportunity where our community comes together and strengthens our connections.

The director of Neighborhood Bridges for Fairhope, Lori Terral, said, "Fairhope is so generous – as soon as I post a need, it gets met. There's no red tape, mountains of paperwork, or embarrassing interviews with the school administrators or government agencies; it's just people in the community doing what they love to do — help."

The success of Neighborhood Bridges lies in its simplicity.

"I need" is met with "I'll give."

When the need is identified, a call is made, then an email is sent, and people respond. The student's name is never divulged. The happy ending usually appears within a few days.

Because our public-school children wear uniforms, there is always a need for specific khaki pants or school-approved shirts. The morning will inevitably arrive when all three children in the family have outgrown their last pair of decent pants, but the budget doesn't allow for a shopping spree for all three.

Lori said, "There's no waste because people are donating to the exact need for the moment." Donors can participate one time only, or repeatedly.

Have we finally returned to common sense?

The City of Fairhope initially adopted and launched the non-profit program. When it quickly spread to include other areas of Baldwin County, private citizens stepped in to oversee the daily operations. Lori Terral handles the needs of Fairhope schools, while others concentrate on monetary donations, transportation, and other schools in nearby Bay Minette, Spanish Fort, Foley, Robertsdale, and Loxley.

Lori told the story of one family that lost everything in a fire. Because of the group's connective aspect, within a few days, Neighborhood Bridges located a family whose elderly mother had passed away, leaving furniture they didn't need and wanted to donate. Another email request identified volunteers who offered to make the pick-up and delivery.

Most requests are small but can make a huge difference to a child's self-image and overall state of mind. New school supplies, a lunchbox, or a warm coat can be an emotional lift. Individually wrapped snacks are a frequent request because it's difficult for a child to watch friends nibble on cookies when they have nothing to satisfy their afternoon hunger. And the flute that your daughter left lying around your house for the last 20 years can suddenly be loved again in the hands of a student just discovering the beauty of music. All it takes is answering an email.

Vetted and approved by the school guidance counselors or other administrators, the needs are always legitimate and within the organization's scope. If a request exceeds the parameters of Neighborhood Bridges, they'll often partner with other organizations for things like temporary emergency housing, help with job searches, or medical crises. "It's a team effort," Lori said.

Transactions of items are anonymous, with donors sometimes dropping things off directly at the school or other volunteers helping with deliveries. "Everyone gets big smiles and thanks from the school staff when they walk in and whisper they're with Neighborhood Bridges."

For many years, the five- and six-year-olds at Fairhope's K-1 Center would stand next to their desks every morning and recite their school motto, "Treat others the way you want to be treated." This version of the Golden Rule is what exemplifies Neighborhood Bridges.

Children have long memories of those who have shown kindness. They may not know the name or face of the person who helped, but the memory of how it felt to be treated with compassion and dignity by a stranger will never be forgotten. I predict that someday they'll be the first in our community to offer mercy to others.

No matter how small or large the gift may be, those who give and those who receive are somehow changed. Their hearts are forever connected by a very special Neighborhood Bridge.

A soldier from Fairhope's National Guard 1165th Police Company arrives home from Afghanistan in December 2011, to the cheers of family and friends at the Fairhope Civic Center.

27

Meanwhile at the Nail Salon

Mattie Mae came flying into the nail salon shrieking, "It's the gospel truth and I swear I heard it myself! The Birmingham people are halfway to their fundraising goal of constructing a new Vulcan to overlook the bay."

She slid into the chair next to her friend, Marybeth, who asked, "Why are so many people from Birmingham moving here?"

"I know! If they love looking at Vulcan buns so much, why don't they just stay put in Birmingham?"

Bian, the owner of the nail salon, said in Vietnamese to her assistant, Diep, "Tại sao họ không muốn người dân Birmingham chuyển đến đây?" (Why don't they want Birmingham people to move here?)

"No, thank you, I'd like Cadillac Pink this time," Marybeth said.

"Have you seen their traffic? It's terrible. That's why they want to live in Fairhope," said Mattie Mae.

"It's no better here these days," Marybeth said as she admired her nails. "It took me 30 minutes to get home from Bunco last night."

"Yeah, now that the Birmingham folks are mixed in with the Atlanta people, there's more traffic here than New York City."

"That's an exaggeration and you know it."

"Well, per square mile, it's absolutely true."

"Look! My toes are so pretty!" said Velda as she wobbled over to the others, being careful not to smudge the Cajun Shrimp orangey tint on her toes.

"But they won't really put up a new Vulcan, will they? I mean, it looks majestic way up on that big mountain, but right here at eye level it will definitely be a bit tacky, don't you think?" said Marybeth with a pout.

"Well, a smaller version is planned, from what I heard," said the all-authoritative Mattie Mae. "But I think he'll be mooning the Marietta Johnson statue if they aren't careful."

Bian said, "Tại sao họ luôn khó chịu vì những điều không bao giờ xảy ra?" (Why do they always get so upset over things that never happen?)

"Why, yes, thank you, I would love a bottle of water," responded Velda.

Then she added, "I wish they'd bring Birmingham barbecue instead of a statue."

Marybeth's eyes lit up as she said, "Saw's or Dreamland? Or wait, Demetri's. That's what they can bring us. I love that stuff."

Mattie Mae held her hand up to admire her shiny, semi-natural, not too gaudy, not too plain nails and said, "Who knows? After Atlanta and Birmingham, I think we're in for an invasion from Tennessee next."

"Never! Tennessee's prettier than down here, and besides, they couldn't take the heat or hurricanes," said Velda.

"Well, my cousin said Nashville's in a tizzy because new folks are moving in by the thousands who don't even know who Johnny Cash was," said Marybeth.

Diep asked Bian, "Bạn có định nói với họ rằng bạn đã tốt nghiệp đứng đầu lớp tại Vestavia Hills ở Birmingham không?" (Are you going to tell them you graduated at the top of your class from Vestavia Hills in Birmingham?)

Bian laughed and said, "Tại sao? Đây là lý do tại sao tôi yêu Fairhope. Những người phụ nữ này điên rồi!" (Why? This is why I love Fairhope. These ladies are crazy!)

The ladies all giggled and said, "Oh, Bian, you have the loveliest laugh!"

28

Let's Give Them Something to Talk About

As I write this, our McDonald's is a pile of rubble. It seems anti-American not to be able to grab a Big Mac whenever you want. From what I've heard, a few McDonald's employees decided to fry their Thanksgiving turkey in the French fry vat of boiling oil, but something went surprisingly wrong, (you saw that coming, right?) which resulted in a massive fire. The Fairhope Volunteer Fire Department responded promptly and extinguished the blaze, only to have it reignite later that day — at least, that's the explanation I heard. It's a small town, so there are twelve other versions of this story floating around, including one that involves a bobcat (the animal, not tractor). We love good stories and have heard them all.

Speaking of Ronald McDonald and the best French fries on earth, let me tell you about Clyde Ingersoll, who owns Ingersoll Air and Heating, who kindly came to our house at 10:30 one night in July to repair our air conditioner. "I couldn't let y'all sleep in this heat," he said. We cut our visit short that evening, but I usually spend a lot of time talking to one of the best storytellers in Fairhope. Clyde was born here in 1952 and grew up on his family's farm, located where McDonald's is now, or at least where it used to be — ahh, there's the McDonald's connection you were waiting for. His daddy also grew up here and farmed on property that extended back to where Blue Island Avenue is now. Clyde weaves excellent stories about his adventures of roaming a town where everyone knew one another and our modern subdivisions were nothing but cool shaded woodlands.

Like most Southerners, Fairhopers are talkers. If we aren't engaged in a specific conversation with someone like Clyde, we're prone to start a conversation with anyone nearby. "Woo! It's too hot to cook," we say to no one in particular in line at the bookstore. Someone responds, "I know, I'm going to The Goat at The Pig to pick up dinner." Another says, "I love The Goat. James makes the best salmon I've ever had." Everyone nods in agreement, then off we go. We all move on.

Newcomers are suspicious but eventually learn we're only making polite conversation aimed at anyone who has ears to hear. It's a game of "toss-up," seeing who will respond.

Let's Give Them Something to Talk About

We talk to everyone because we've been raised in tight-knit communities where we know if we speak to someone, we may discover the connection that ties the man at the store to a cousin who owned the gas station where our best friend's father worked as a teenager.

That's where those new to the South must take a deep breath and either join in or risk being "aloof." And believe me, being aloof leads down the dreaded path to being "discussed."

"I have that same blouse," said a woman who was passing me at Fairhope Pharmacy.

"J.Crew?" I asked.

"Yes." She nodded.

"I just love it and get so many compliments when I wear it."

"Me too!"

Then she added, "You look really cute in it."

"I'm sure you do, too."

We both gave little laughs and continued walking in opposite directions, smiling at our new momentary friendship. We shared an entire conversation and found something in common, yet that was it. Done. Gone. Exited forever from each other's lives. And yet, we both felt somehow nourished in a way only friends can make us feel.

The invention of wireless earbuds has caused great confusion in the South. Those who wear them for a phone conversation without actually holding the phone to their ear appear to be talking to everyone, yet they're isolated in their own world of privacy. This exasperates the rest of us. They chatter away and expect us to know they aren't talking to us.

Don't they understand how general chit-chat works?

I once ran into the late retired pastor, Marcus Smith, in Piggly Wiggly, and he laughed and said, "I talked to that young man over there for a full minute before I realized he was talking into space or into an earpiece, or whatever it was."

I laughed and said, "I know, it's weird."

"He may be a spy," Marcus joked.

"But I'll bet you invited him to church," I guessed.

Let's Give Them Something to Talk About

"Of course I did, but I think he only got half of what I said, so he may end up down the street with the Baptists."

The lady sitting next to us in the dentist's office waiting room may have been the sister of our son's fourth-grade teacher, and I'm pretty sure the man holding the door open for me at Saraceno's is the uncle of one of my book club friends. We assume we're connected to at least one person thumping watermelons at the farmer's market, so it's okay to say, "These look so much better than last year's crop." And sure enough, everyone responds in the affirmative.

In butterfly moments as brief as a flutter and quick as a flap, we share concern. "Oh, you poor thing. I've had to wear a boot on my broken foot before and know how uncomfortable it is." We're also quick to offer tips. "If you want the Royal Reds, hold on, they're unloading the fresh ones in a minute."

Our slow drawl in regular conversations is often abbreviated for passing strangers.

"Didja ever put one in the microwave?" someone asked over Felicity Jean's shoulder. She was holding a box of MoonPies and curiously turned to see a face she didn't recognize. "Just a few seconds is all it takes to puff 'em up." Then, as quickly as he appeared, the MoonPie connoisseur was gone.

Many lifelong friends started their relationships with casual words on the playground. "I like your Hot Wheels." Or as adults standing on the original location of Clyde's family farm and lamenting to no one in particular, "Is it too much to ask that the milkshake machine work just once?"

Whether we're friends forever or friendly for a moment, it's yet another way we connect. That's not such a bad thing, is it?

Feel free to answer aloud. Someone will surely respond.

29

Food, Nutrition and Kindness

If barbecue and sweet tea could cure disease, we'd live forever. But like most Southerners, we tune out warnings from our doctors because we will always love fried catfish with sides of baked brown sugar beans and buttery cheese grits.

We're a region where food is brought to our house the day we're born and again the day we die. The meals in between are both memorable and forgotten, and sadly, nutrition is usually an afterthought.

But an enthusiastic group of Fairhopers, including doctors, hospital administrators, and philanthropists Louis and Melinda Mapp, have asked, "What if our food could heal and prevent disease?" In keeping with our city's spirit of creative innovation, The Teaching Kitchen opened in Fairhope in early 2023. As part of the University of South Alabama Mapp Family Campus, the professionally equipped kitchen space is designed for research, recipe development, and in-person instruction.

The sweeping top-floor view from the bright windows of the kitchen ironically overlooks a former peanut field where, in years past, local Baldwin County farmers sold sweet potatoes from the back of their trucks. Of course, peanuts and sweet potatoes bring to mind another Alabama food scientist, Tuskegee University's George Washington Carver, who would be amazed and delighted with this new generation's research and instruction.

Cooking classes will be offered to culinary staff members from schools, senior living facilities, restaurants, and anyone interested in learning more about healthy food options.

Although teaching people in Alabama how to cook may seem like teaching water to be wet, everyone seems to understand that no matter how delicious they are, the biscuits and gravy we've always loved aren't the keys to longevity.

Unlocking preparation techniques for foods we've previously ignored or discarded may enable us to reverse, prevent, or even heal illnesses and diseases we've sadly grown to accept as part of aging.

Food, Nutrition and Kindness

Louis and Melinda Mapp have been generous, quiet, and humble supporters of the Fairhope community, and there are many others just like them who serve behind the scenes, taking care of needs that arise. When Louis was in his 80s, he drove to Mobile to nurture and rock premature babies every week at the University of South Alabama Women's and Children's Birthing Center. The connections he made with these infants will never be remembered by the babies, but those in Fairhope who know his story have been inspired to reach out to others in their own way. Age isn't an issue when you're plugged into the place where your gifts and passions connect.

Previously, the Mapps' kindness was shown when they stepped in to help Fairhope's National Guard 1165th Police Company, which had finally arrived home from Afghanistan but was being held for processing in Hattiesburg, Mississippi.

Days of bureaucratic paperwork dragged on, and soon everyone realized there was a problem securing government transportation for the trip back to Fairhope.

With Christmas just days away, it looked like the 170 soldiers would miss another holiday with their families.

With hearts full of the Christmas spirit, not to mention great common sense, Louis and Melinda arranged for private charter buses to retrieve the soldiers and deliver them 114 miles into the arms of their loved ones in Fairhope, just in time for Christmas Day.

It was one of the happiest days in our city I can remember. Crowds of Fairhopers lined the streets with "welcome home" signs and waved American flags. The city's hook and ladder truck suspended a giant American flag over Section Street, and as the buses passed beneath, children jumped around and held signs welcoming their fathers and mothers home. Family, friends, and strangers simultaneously cried and laughed and hugged each other at the happy homecoming.

When I think about how the people in Fairhope come together with their different resources, ages, and experience to make things work, I'm reminded of "Stone Soup." This old fable tells the story of a town where everyone contributed whatever meager item they had until the pot was filled with a delicious soup. One gave his last potato, another brought an onion, and another a carrot — until finally, the simmering pot smelled wonderful and was ready to feed and nourish the entire community.

With all the gifts and efforts of people like the Mapps, who inspire others to use their gifts, Fairhope will always have a delicious pot of soup, and I'm pretty sure it will be healthy.

30

Infrastructure

If you've watched old movies featuring Audrey Hepburn perched on the back of a Vespa zipping past ruins, you're sure to have noticed the traffic circles. These busy hubs have been a fixture in ancient civilizations and cause no alarm to the sophisticated Europeans. However, in the last few years, we've added a few smaller traffic circles, or "roundabouts," in Fairhope, and they've caused a literal small-town stir.

The Roman soldiers steered their chariots around the curves, thus avoiding time-consuming traffic lights. Now, their modern tiny cars, taxis, scooters, and buses smoothly glide side by side in a space with no marked lanes whatsoever, and pedestrians somehow meander through the swirling chaos unscathed.

Locally, our Fords and Chevys ignore the "keep moving" signs and come to a screeching halt the first time they approach the simple one-lane circle. "What in the tarnation?" "How do we get on it?" "Which way do we go?" "Did my tax money pay for this?" "Look at the cows!"

"Alfred! Keep going! The cars behind us are tooting their horns."

"They're just saying howdy."

The first weekend the original roundabout opened on Fairhope Avenue and County Road 13, I saw two young men in a small pick-up truck, with bare feet dangling out the passenger side window and their fishing poles swaying in the back bed. Hoots of laughter came from within as the truck zipped around and around – four times in total, as I watched from my rear-view mirror and probably more as I drove away. In a small town, these roundabouts are the most exciting thing to happen since we started watching the city council meetings on live stream.

Lots of signage with directions on how to use the roundabout detract from the simplistic beauty of the elegant swirling path. A chunk of cement curb in the center is already knocked out of place where someone decided to save time by cutting straight across the middle.

Infrastructure

In the olden pre-roundabout days, I often took this road to my son's school in the mornings. There was a dangerously ignored four-way stop, and many mornings I was blinded by glaring sun or heavy fog. Even more dangerous were the chivalrous Southern gentlemen who arrived at the intersection first but insisted, "You go first." "No!" I'd shake my head. "Follow the traffic rules and just go!" They'd smile and gently try to wave me through while people behind the nice man were agitated because he wouldn't take his rightful turn. I adore good manners, but a four-way stop isn't the place for gentility. Roundabouts restore practicality and, like collard greens, keep things moving.

In full confession, I was pulled over one evening by a Fairhope police officer who claimed I was going a "bit too fast, ma'am" around the roundabout. The days have passed since I could use innocent youth as a way to avoid a ticket, so this time I tried hopeless honesty. "I'm so sorry, but I'm on my way home from tennis lessons at Stimpson Field (they're free to Fairhope residents), where I just played, and by the way, actually beat women half my age. I'm exhausted and just want to get home and rest." I detest competition, and our tennis instructor had us playing without keeping score — but come now, if you are killing it, you secretly keep score in your head. The young officer noticed my breathless motherly charm. The kind young man took pity and said I could go with no ticket. The full confessional truth is, I may have possibly been taking a celebratory victory lap around the roundabout with a little "We Are the Champions" blast of Queen on the stereo. I mean, come on, those women were half my age.

We now have four roundabouts, with yet another planned near St. James Episcopal Church. This is indeed a tricky intersection, with misaligned roads, a distracting tick-tock clock made of flowers, and open-minded Christians zooming off to Sunday brunch.

It's like the Daytona 500 around here now, with Grandma cutting in front of the school bus as it goes round and round and sways to the side, almost leaning on two wheels to keep out of the way of the monster truck following behind. I never thought there would be so much excitement driving through the bucolic scenery of Alabama farmland. But here we go, finally getting around to bigger and better things.

Much to my fascination, the city has also incorporated visual tricks and illusions to slow downtown traffic, such as adding trees to the medians that evoke a watermelon color scheme in the summer and creating "bump outs" of flower beds along the edges of the streets. The most interesting has been the widening of the actual painted lines along the edges of the roads. Does it really fool us into slowing down? Yes. I'm baffled by my gullibility but impressed with the city's manipulation of optical illusions. We slow from 20 miles per hour to a creeping 15, which in turn makes us slow down and yeah . . . smell the flowers.

We fear, with the exploding growth in our area, that our cornfield intersections will soon rival the congested and crazy Roman Piazza Venezia,

Infrastructure

but for now, the cows get a kick out of watching us spin out of control on a circular path. We feel sophisticated in a slow, roundabout sort of way.

Owning a business in downtown Fairhope for over 50 years hasn't always been easy, but I've held to the belief that "no man is an island." The personal connections with wonderful employees, customers, city leaders, and neighboring business owners have all contributed to our success and the vibrant atmosphere of our downtown.
—**Ann Miller,** co-founder (with husband Marc) of M&F Casuals

31

Here's a Bit of Advice

Lucy van Pelt has been replaced. Her "psychiatric help" booth Charlie Brown often visited has been updated for the better since Sonya and Nancye opened their advice booth in our local bookstore. Every Tuesday, friends and strangers come to Page and Palette, sip a cup of coffee, and wait their turn for (almost) free advice from two sage women. Sitting behind a rickety plywood booth that looks just like the one from Peanuts, the women put their talents together to offer words of wisdom to our community. For almost 10 years now, the insightful duo has met their customers and matched cartoon Lucy's fee of 5 cents per session. All donations go to the tip jar for the young baristas making the coffee and serving muffins.

Sonya Bennett and Nancye Jennings recognized they shared a passion and gift for listening to other's problems and developed a plan to help the community. Knowing they had experience with just about everything, they presented their idea to Page and Palette owner Karin Wilson, who said, "Why not give it a try?"

At first, some thought the advice booth was too immature, silly, or flat-out weird, but after they tried it, they found themselves deeply entranced with the wisdom and kindness of the "advice ladies."

A man in his late 20s could be seen talking with the duo last week. He had to slump down in his chair a bit to peer beneath the overhead hand-painted plywood "Friendly Advice" header. Nancye nodded in agreement with what he was saying, and Sonya offered quiet words that must have hit the target because a huge smile spread across the customer's face. Was he seeking career advice? Or perhaps he was wondering about the best way to propose to his longtime girlfriend. Who knows? It's all confidential.

When I first visited the advice booth, I thought I would humor myself and get a good story for my newspaper column, but then they asked me to choose a card from a deck and read it aloud. "Oh, I get it, it's one of those hocus-pocus card tricks you see in Jackson Square in New Orleans that my Sunday School teacher warned me about," I thought. But after reading the card, which wasn't hocus-pocus at all, Sonya and Nancye asked a very practical question: "What do you think about reliability?"

Here's a Bit of Advice

After a brief exchange of ideas, they asked if anything was on my mind. "Oh no, nothing really," I replied. But then, I reconsidered and said, "You know, there is this one thing that keeps bothering me..." and suddenly, we were off to the races. With motherly tenderness and the sharpness of an expert witness, they helped pinpoint the source of stress and gave their thoughts on coping. It was much more detailed than when my friends say, "Well honey, WWJSD," or, "What would Julia Sugarbaker do?"

With their collective experiences of teaching, parenting, and community service, the Fairhope Advice Ladies embody a wealth of wisdom. Their calming presence has become a springboard for many great ideas, relationships, and adventures. Sometimes it's nice to have someone sit and listen to what's on your heart. And for only a nickel, it's totally worth the price.

The duck pond area, not as developed as it is today, was once considered a nude beach. The Fairhope Museum of History has a photo of a family standing on their heads there, buck naked. In the 1930s, the neighboring Daphne City Council announced that Fairhopers would not be welcome at their Mayday celebrations because they didn't want naked people showing up. One woman in town (name redacted because her family still lives here), who was a known nudist, burned herself while canning pears, so she gave the practice up and returned to wearing clothes.
— **Donald Hatchett Barrett**, native Fairhoper, city historian, and first tea farmer in the United States

32

The Pandemic

I get queasy just thinking about this topic, but if I'm honestly assessing our community, this plays a big part in recent history, if not the central role in our moods and current state of mind.

We thought we lived in an untouchable utopian bubble. Sheltered from the rest of the hurried, frazzled world, we relaxed by the bay and sipped sweet tea. And then, we heard of a virus sweeping through Italy.

Like other small towns in America, we watched in disbelief as it eventually spread to our country and then our communities.

Whatever I say here will be controversial because the political climate of the entire country at this time is still one of anger, mistrust, and confusion. Everyone is on edge, and fear of offense seems never-ending.

In April 2020, a local doctor was one of the first Fairhopers to contract Coronavirus, later known as "Covid-19." It was such big news that J.D. Crowe of *The Mobile Press-Register* wrote a full-page story on the doctor's experience. The patient recovered, but unfortunately, within months, the virus had become far more common and, confusingly, seemed to affect each person differently.

Facial masks that covered our noses and mouths were required in public, which some say resulted in preventing the spread of the virus, while others say were useless and created more controversy. Wearing or not wearing a mask became a political statement and spurred heated arguments.

In my opinion, the most irritating and worthless effort was placing directional arrows on the floors of grocery stores. One-way traffic patterns were supposed to prevent people from crossing paths, but you still had to pass slow shoppers, and no one remembered to follow the arrows anyway, which led to more bafflement and irritation.

"Social distancing" was the new phrase we heard everywhere and one of total confusion for talkative, sociable Southerners. While half the town was panicking over being in close proximity to others, the other half was

The Pandemic

hyperventilating and having cold sweats from not being able to visit their people.

All clubs and meetings were canceled because everyone was encouraged and often required to stay home. Sociable small-town Southerners were losing their minds. The great dividing lines became more pronounced as job loss was a huge concern for some while others worried about losing their housekeepers.

Covering the mouths of Southerners and limiting their ability to congregate caused great angst. We're talkers, smilers, greeters, whistlers, and "yes ma'am"-ers and "no-sir"-ers. We felt bound and gagged.

Public schools were closed for several months, and classes were held via computer when possible. When the schools finally reopened, children and teachers were required to wear masks, which interfered with vital communication. As with all types of hardships, the youngest were traumatized the most. It was an exhausting year for everyone, and many experienced teachers took this as an opportunity to retire.

There were days when Downtown Fairhope looked like an eerie ghost town. Every bed at Thomas Hospital was full, and elective surgeries were canceled. 3 Circle Church held drive-thru clinics to test for the virus. Dressed in hazmat-looking suits, they leaned through the car windows and poked giant Q-tips in people's noses. Other churches offered drive-thru vaccines. "We're here to help, but whatever you do, just don't get out of your car and come near us — peace be with you and bless you, my child." Even doctor's offices offered drive-thru services to lessen human contact. Those in the know knew where to find drive-thru margaritas.

Fear, anger, irritation, depression, and outrage fueled online conversations. The decision to get vaccinated or not was as hotly debated as the wearing of masks. Sadly, the different opinions split friendships and families.

When churches in Alabama were banned from opening their doors on Easter Sunday, we felt like hell was bubbling over. How could this happen to the entire world, much less our perfectly protected and seemingly insulated small town? Everyone was stunned.

Then, the Fairhope spirit awakened.

Earlier than most cities, Fairhope tapped into our bottomless well of creativity. Connections proved too strong to be forgotten, and citizens acted quickly to care for others. Calling those who lived alone to check on them or dropping off supplies to older neighbors who couldn't venture out, people found new ways to stay in touch while supporting their friends and neighbors who owned local businesses.

The Pandemic

In June of 2020, the entire town was buzzing with excitement when country music star Alan Jackson announced he would hold two socially distanced drive-in, stay-in-your-truck concerts. One event was in beautiful (and also rapidly growing) Cullman, Alabama, and the other was right here in Fairhope.

Two thousand vehicles waited in traffic for more than three hours to enter the field at Oak Hollow Farms, where trucks and cars parked a safe six feet apart. Encouraged to remain near our vehicles, some couldn't resist the temptation of a good fist fight as both women and men threw punches and rolled across the hoods of trucks. Someone blew their Dukes of Hazzard horn repeatedly until things calmed down. To say people were a bit stir-crazy is an understatement. Alan Jackson's music soothed the savage crowd, and I'm sure Paul, the mail carrier, was busy the next day delivering notes of apology.

Ever the optimist that things would quickly return to normal — "any day now, I'm sure," — I ordered a dress from my favorite downtown shop, M&F Casuals, and found it delivered to my porch later that day with a kind note of thanks. Confinement isn't quite so bad while sporting a new frock. Others had the same idea and began calling local businesses and doing what they could to help.

We were all a hot mess of one variety or the other. I bounced back and forth, crying and pleading with God to heal my friend Sherry, who was terribly sick, but then cursed the stupid people on TV telling me to wipe down my mail before it came into the house.

Amid the chaos and confusion, Fairhope bounced back to life. Business owners strategized, friends and neighbors planned, and everyone put their heads together (virtually) to form a new way of life. We were still small enough to know one another and recognized the importance of keeping our downtown businesses afloat.

Closing churches in Alabama was like closing casinos in Las Vegas — wait a minute, I think they actually did close the casinos. It was indeed a bizarre time. And for those who worshiped in the stadiums, the ACC, SEC, and Big 12 played their college football games to nearly empty stands while the other conferences postponed their seasons altogether.

No football or church in Alabama made us feel like we were living on the moon. They may as well have outlawed grits and banned the "y'all's."

In true *Braveheart* Scottish style, Eastern Shore Presbyterian Church was early to devise a determined and safe plan for meeting in person. After a few weeks of being closed, they creatively mapped out a way to use the large campus, broadcasting their services from the main sanctuary into the gymnasium and other big rooms. With plenty of options to spread out, most members felt comfortable returning to one form or the other of in-person worship. Other churches soon followed, yet others sadly remained closed for a year.

Tamara Wintzell, the owner of Tamara's Downtown restaurant, was the first restaurateur to offer curbside service. Tamara recalls, "The Alabama Department of Health mandated all restaurants in the state close for sit-down service on a Sunday, so I thought about it all night, and Monday morning started feeding customers curbside." Tamara added, "We hit upon a system where people could call their order in, then pull their cars up in front of the restaurant, and we'd hand it to them through the window." She remembered, "Family-sized lasagna and fried chicken saved my restaurant and kept every one of my employees on the payroll." She laughed about how, as a bonus, she occasionally threw in a free roll of coveted and hard-to-find toilet paper with the order.

Other restaurants and businesses soon followed with curbside pick-ups, and their loyal customers and friends did their best to keep commerce moving.

The city noticed the curbside trend and created official "pick-up zones" on the street. Parking in the green-striped spaces allowed you to stay just long enough to pick up food, a pharmacy order, or a new book. Minimal contact was important yet remained a nuisance.

The situation continued much longer than anyone thought possible. People grew frustrated and lonely for human contact. Our small town felt broken.

I'm sure past wars and the Great Depression touched Fairhope in memorable ways. I remember the terrorist attacks of September 11, 2001, when every house and seemingly all the cars and trucks displayed American flags. We were a small town united in deep patriotism. Our community was undivided then, but Covid had the opposite effect. For the first time we could remember, Fairhope was torn apart.

We're still sorting out what should have or could have been done differently. And while there are still plenty of hotly debated opinions, the one point of agreement is that no one ever wants this to happen again. Seeing Fairhope and larger America divided, angry, and fearful was one of the worst times in our national and local history.

Here is a newspaper column I wrote when the shut-down was relatively new, that expressed the sadness we were feeling. Little did I know, the situation was only beginning and would continue for at least another full year.

The Pandemic

A Golden Glimmer of Hope
First published in *The Mobile Press-Register*, *Birmingham News*, and *Huntsville Times*
June 2020, only two months into the Covid 19 ordeal

Like a disco ball at the skating rink, I know it's tacky, but it's still just so pretty, I can't stop looking. There's a speck of glitter embedded in my living room rug, left over from Christmas, and for some weird reason, I love it.

As I swish around the house at night, cutting off the lights, there it is. At the end of the sofa, in front of the fireplace, glimmering gold. Always too tired to mess with it at night, I make a mental note to deal with it later, yet when I return to search during daylight hours, discover it's no longer visible.

Days, weeks, and now months of trying to free the one speck of glitter have proven useless because every night, in the perfectly lit beam of the lamp, there it is. Still a reminder of December days and tidings of comfort and joy that seem a million years ago.

The COVID-19 virus and the agitated world in which we live are surreal and filled with so many sick, angry, sad, and lonely people. We're cut off from those we love, and even though we may not be officially depressed, we're taking on the qualities of those who are overwhelmed with sadness. Overeating, oversleeping, and heavy hearts are the result of weddings that have been canceled and funerals postponed. Family reunions are on hold;

we can't cuddle new babies, and who knows what will happen with schools this fall?

That exact spot on the rug has been vacuumed 5,000 times by my staff (my son, who is home from college), and yet, the minuscule sparkle appears again every night. I feel the festive speck has exhibited such deep determination to cling to our family that it deserves a place of honor and should be allowed to remain.

The true reason I don't get up right now and go on a complete search-and-destroy mission for the glitter is really because that microscopic gleam of gold actually makes me happy. It's a reminder of the peace and fun we shared last December and maybe even a literal glimmer of hope for a normal holiday season yet to come.

If one spot of glitter on my rug gives me a split second to remember the last time the world felt orderly and we were all together celebrating, then it's okay with me to leave it there. Probably shaken from the Christmas tree while I was packing away the ornaments while watching bowl games and finishing off the last of the Christmas cookies, it's a nightly reminder that things were once normal, happy, and sparkly.

Here we are at the beginning of hurricane season, and I'm finding comfort in a single speck of leftover Christmas glitter. It's getting warmer and muggier outside, and the humidity is already thick. Yet there, on the

The Pandemic

rug, if I tip my head just right and squint my eyes as I reach for the lamp, there is the most glorious happy sparkle that somehow links me to a time when everyone was home, no one was sick, our businesses were booming, and there were glittery ornaments on the tree.

The Old Fairhope City Hall is now used as the Fairhope Museum of History and hosts special events like the Elderberry Festival.

33

Alligators in the Bay

As my three-year old son dug holes in the sand on the edge of Mobile Bay, something in the water caught my eye. I shielded my face from the sun and squinted to see two dark beady eyes surface about 20 feet from shore. The eyes submerged then popped back up a few feet closer. As my snack-sized son moved along the beach, the alligator eyes followed, back and forth, moving left then right. It wasn't the relaxing day I'd planned, so we hiked back up the bluff and went home.

Yes, there are alligators in and around Mobile Bay. They've followed kayakers, snatched small pets, and even stalked picnicking couples. Geese at the public duck pond are feathery feasts for the leathery beasts. Tourists find alligators interesting, but locals know their devious side and stay away.

After that encounter, I was always mindful of the stealthy beasts slithering near the Bay. I know the argument; we built our city in their habitat, and they have first right of refusal on anything edible, yet we want to share. Our share should be wherever we are, and their share should be far away from that.

Many of you will understand that as my sons grew older, keeping them away from the area where the alligators rollicked and roiled became difficult. My sons and the mama alligator's sons shared the same curiosity and natural habitat. She was probably just as fearful of my sons as I was of hers, but the allure of the shared play space was so enticing; what was I to do? Generations of Fairhope children have played in the gullies and along the bay, and several of my older friends told me it was perfectly safe to allow my sons to "roam" the town. After all, it's what made them such incredible adults. "A childhood in Fairhope is wasted if the boys sit inside all day." Finding that to be true of just about any town, I agreed.

My husband and I decided to let the boys roam free, but only after giving them strict safety instructions of "don't poke the gators, and run like heck in a zig-zag pattern if they chase you." That slows them down, right? Well, no. Try climbing a tree instead.

No matter what, the number-one thing that equipped them to handle the dangerous, toothy predator was prayer. A mother's prayers are the most potent tool against childhood mishaps. So, it was up to me to keep them safe.

The boys explored kudzu-tangled gullies and swamps equipped with Indiana Jones-style boots, pocketknives, insect repellent, a yapping dog, and big sticks. They found and dissected owl pellets and made rope swings from overhanging limbs. After romping all day, my sons would return home with blackberry-stained lips, scratched knees, and a fist full of weeds for me to put in a vase.

One evening, my husband and I joined the boys on a walk to the bay. Crossing the swamp on a homemade wobbly boardwalk consisting of two warped boards, the boys led me to their favorite spot to watch the sunset. Just as the sky turned purple, we heard an alligator give a loud "grumph-harumph!" — yes, that's the only way I know how to explain it in writing. In person, I could give you a much better impersonation. My husband said it was no big deal, but it haunted me all night.

The next day, I bravely walked down the wooded path to the bay on my own, and sure enough, as I came within sight of the water, I heard the alligator again. Arriving home at a record speed, I called the Department of Alabama Wildlife Services, who redirected me to two other offices before someone took my call.

"Yes, hello?"

"Hi, I live in Fairhope and need to let you know about an alligator that's in the middle of a populated area where neighborhood children play."

I could hear the man sigh as if I were the 14th overly concerned mother he'd talked to that day.

"Excuse me, ma'am, but have you seen this alligator yourself?"

"No, but I heard it."

"How do you know what an alligator sounds like?"

"I grew up along the Gulf Coast and just know these sort of things."

"Yes, ma'am, I understand. So, how exactly does this alligator sound to you?"

"Like a 300-pound frog." And then I gave him my dead-ringer impersonation of "grumph – harumph!"

"Ummm, we'll be out later this afternoon."

"Uh-huh. I thought so."

Alligators in the Bay

Two game officials arrived, and the boys and I pointed them toward the alligator's evil lair. After about 30 minutes, they returned and said they had indeed located the gator, and although he was larger than expected, he was still too small to relocate.

"You'd rather move a large alligator than a small one?"

"Yes, ma'am. That's how it works."

Does any part of the government make sense?

So I did what I'm called to do; I started praying the official prayer for protection from modern-day beady-eye dinosaurs. I think I originally read it in the back of the Broadman Hymnal. When I was finished, that was one prayed-over and confused alligator.

Exactly one week later, Hurricane Ivan blew through town, taking down buildings, trees, and power lines and washing away the alligator. We don't know where he went, but he was never heard from again.

See you later, scary gator. Prayers from moms are even greater.

The thing I love about living in Fairhope is that if I don't really know what I am doing, someone else certainly does.
— **Tammy Wintzell**, owner of Tamara's Downtown restaurant

34

Barbecue is Not an Event

Barring the arrival of insects the size of Volkswagens, storms the size of Manhattan, and humidity that arrives by tanker truck, we love to eat outdoors. The first coffin to be used for burial in the Colony Cemetery was actually constructed from a picnic table. A riparian feast followed by a bayside funeral: the Founders knew how to make the best of everything.

Here's a list of popular ways Fairhopers turn food into an outdoor social event.

Cook-out — This is the act of grilling food and usually involves hamburgers, hot dogs, or steaks. Alabama-made Conecuh sausage is also very popular on the grill. We love to grill seafood, and come to think of it, much like frying, we'll grill almost anything we can shoot, hook, or trap.

Barbecue (BBQ) — This should never ever- ever be confused with the above "cook-out." A barbecue is not an event; it's a serious food category. If you invite someone from the South over for "barbecue" and give them hamburgers, you'll be blackballed from social events for a minimum of two years, and your children will be pitied. Being discussed will be the least of your worries. Fairhopers rarely mess around with North Alabama white sauce, not that we don't like it, it's just their thing, not ours. Our red sauce version is strong and tangy with a hint of sweetness. Sounds like my husband.

With pork or chicken slow-cooking all day, lines form early at the BBQ joint du jour. Do-it-yourself recipes for the perfect BBQ sauce are a guarded secret passed down through generations, and home cooks who master the art of BBQ sometimes turn professional and win trophies for their efforts. Jack Powell is one of the best BBQ connoisseurs in town and donates much of his time and the use of his enormous smoker to charity events. He can tell you all about heating methods, meat selections, temperatures, and sauce recipes. If high school had included a class called "The Science of Outdoor Cooking," Jack would have been the valedictorian.

Sean Miller is the champion of brisket, and my late friend Alan Harper was a professional BBQ judge who studied and learned to identify excellent barbecue. He took his job seriously and was just getting ready to give me some insider tips when he passed on to heaven, where I'm sure he oversees the saints' feast prepared for those who hunger for righteous "Q."

Fish fry — This involves a large outdoor cauldron of boiling oil. Catfish are a favorite to fry, as are local mullet, but only if caught the same day, usually by cast net. If you invite me to a good fish fry that includes baked beans and real hushpuppies (not dense, frozen balls of doom), I'll keep your children while you're on an extended vacation. Throw in coleslaw, and I'll also water your plants.

Low Country boil – This uses another large pot filled with seasoned boiling water and ingredients such as new potatoes from your garden, corn from your friend's farm, and shrimp from the boat docked nearby. Once again, some add the local touch of Conecuh sausage. Whether it's all dipped into individual bowls or spread on a newspaper on the picnic table, this becomes as much of an activity as a delicious meal.

Crawfish boil – Much like the Low Country boil, but take out all the good things and add hard-to-peel mudbugs. Can you tell I'm not a fan? Although a crawfish boil is one of my favorite social activities. There's little to eat, but the tedious peeling process lends more time for laughing and talking.

Oysters – wear a big glove to protect your hand from the lethal knife and just shuck 'em and eat 'em. Lemon, cocktail or hot sauce, and saltine crackers are all that's needed. It's the only time slurping is socially encouraged. The tasty bivalves are yet another thing we can toss on the grill.

Dinner on the grounds — Hold my pocketbook; this may take a while. Dinner on the grounds is a dying art being killed by lazy people or those raised by mothers who are from faraway places – oh, don't clutch your pearls, you know it's true. Are these people young? New to town? Old? Busy? Bad cooks? Who knows, but it seems no one wants to put forth the effort to contribute to the most glorious food event you'll ever experience. Dinner on the grounds is a "potluck" meal held on the church property (grounds), not on the actual dirty ground. Everyone brings their specialty and favorite family dish. It's their moment to shine.

I give thanks every day for belonging to a church that still sings real hymns and has good cooks. When I see that long table swaying under the weight of pies and hams, I channel my inner Julie Andrews and hum, "For somewhere in my youth, or childhood, I must have done something good."

If the church has a permanent cement table or picnic pavilion installed behind the Sunday School building, you know it's a church that is blessed with the gift of culinary excellence, and they value the ties that bind.

If you must bring store-bought food, then we want to wish you a speedy recovery, but please remember to remove it from the store-bought container and place it on a pretty platter — not to be fancy or showy, but to make it pretty. Life is better when everything is pretty. Knowing this, God created flowers, rainbows, big-eyed children, and buttercream icing because he knew our hearts would bubble over with joy at the sight of prettiness. If your dinner on the grounds can somehow manage to incorporate all of the above — flowers, rainbows, big eyes, and buttercream — into the same day, then heaven is truly near.

A wise church food committee chairman is more powerful than the pastor search committee chairman and would never make food assignments according to the first letter of your last name. That's a new invention created by someone who wears white sandals to Thanksgiving dinner and raves about Tim Hortons.

Assigning Mrs. Jackson to bring a vegetable dish when everyone knows she's the four-time county fair winner for pound cake is a disappointment to the entire congregation. Or why, in tarnation, would you force Rondaleigh to bring a plate of meat when she's a vegetarian and can create culinary art out of pinto beans?

Assigning dishes is either a sign that a church lacks faith or someone is a bossy-pants.

There are always those who give the disciple Thomas a run for his position of doubter-in-chief by worrying, "What if no one brings vegetables?" "Will there be enough chicken?" "What if we run out of dessert?" "Who's bringing the dumplings?" "Don't forget to make peanut butter sandwiches for the spoiled children who refuse to eat real food."

The mature women, who have lived through this sort of hand-wringing for decades, snap their apron bows into crisp loops and remind the young worriers, "The miracle of the loaves and fishes fed a crowd of Biblical proportions and was our example of trusting God to supply our needs."

The loaves and fishes is the story of the first-ever dinner on the grounds. We're pretty sure the Hebrew "barley" translates to modern "hushpuppies" and is a role model set before us for all church dinners that were, will be, and are yet to come. "Have faith, my daughters, that all will be well and no one will go home hungry."

Having twelve desserts, five bowls of field peas, four Jell-O molds, nine skillets of cornbread, three sliced watermelons, double bowls of butterbeans, two platters of pear halves topped with Duke's and a cherry, next to nine plates of deviled eggs (all on proper deviled egg plates, of course), and all the ham, chicken and wild rice casseroles, fried chicken, lasagna, and tuna casseroles you can hold is a sign of God's love for us. Who cares if no one thought to bring Copper Coin Carrots? Who cares if we run short on desserts? (Maybe it's God's message to slow down on the sweets).

We'll just make a note to bring more banana pudding next year, and it will all work out. It's a lesson in trust, faith, and fun.

Like us, dinner on the grounds is never perfect, but it gives us a literal taste of our perfect glory yet to come.

Basic picnic on the bay — Many nights, my husband and I will put our dinner in a basket and head to the bay. Thanks to the foresight of city founders, Fairhope has several miles of waterfront parkland where anyone can picnic. When times were tight, my husband and I celebrated our anniversary on the bluff while overlooking the bay and sitting on a quilt made by my great-grandmother. We dined on lobsters steamed by the Delchamps seafood department earlier in the day. Our sons were busy with Wednesday night church activities, so we didn't even need to hire a babysitter. It was one of our favorite anniversaries and one of the prettiest sunsets we've ever seen.

Two months after moving to Fairhope (knowing no one here) it was Mardi Gras season. We attended our first parade, and in addition to the regular candy and beads tossed by the krewes, our daughters also caught warm McDonald's hamburgers, wrapped and sealed in plastic baggies. They thought that was the best thing in the world, and from that moment on, we were sold on Fairhope.

— **Dee Washington,** Fairhope Film Festival Programmer & Steering Committee Member

35

A Dream Come True

J.D. Crowe is Alabama Media Group's political cartoonist. His pointed cartoons have kept us laughing, fuming, and pondering issues for decades. Based on his political targets, I think J.D. and I may be on opposite sides of many, but not all, issues. In true Fairhope style, we don't know for sure because we've never discussed politics. We always find 120 other things to talk about, and I find friends like him to be quite endearing and refreshing for this very reason.

Here's what J.D. had to say about how he came to live in Fairhope. It's familiar to many who have experienced the same dream.

Even though he'd never been to Alabama, J.D. arrived in Mobile in the spring of 2000 to interview for the cartoonist job with the *Mobile Press-Register*. Afterward, he set out to see the beach in Gulf Shores but wandered into a recurring dream along the way.

He recalled, *And then I came upon the flower-lined streets of the little town of Fairhope. Eastern Shore Arts Center on the left. Check. Love me some arts. Old-fashion drugstore downtown on the corner – check. Bookstore in the center of town – check. Ice cream shop – check. Old hardware store with rocking chairs and porch swings outside on the sidewalk – check. Good Lord, I had found Mayberry on the Bluff. And then I drove down to the bay on Mobile Street, through the canopy of live oaks and – overwhelmed with déjà vu – I pulled over at the Orange Avenue Pier. I had been having recurring dreams of this place! The oak trees, the water, the cannons overlooking the bay at the American Legion Hall were especially familiar. I felt ... at home.*

I had been driving around for about two or three hours by this point and thought, "I don't know how far a drive this is from Mobile, but if I get this job, I want to live here."

Twenty-three years later, we still live in the house we bought a few blocks up the street from where I parked that day.

Since then, I have heard from several other folks who just happened to drive through Fairhope and then decided to pick up and move here

A Dream Come True

That's all fine and good, to a point. But enough is enough. We're getting too crowded. Now I think it's time to make a mandatory detour route around Fairhope, especially for folks just out driving around.

We're all glad J.D.'s dream came true.

Photographer Chris Riley enjoys the sunset on Mobile Bay with his dog Tonya.

36

This Little Light of Mine

If you are blessed with a proper porch that sits bayside, street side, farm side, suburban side, or any other side, you know how quickly it becomes a way of life to sit with others, or even alone, to contemplate the world while resting beneath the coolness of the required haint-blue rafters. A ceiling fan or afternoon breeze cools the air, shoos the bugs, and makes it possible to enjoy the outdoors even on the hottest days. Our winters are mild enough that we can sometimes curl up with a big blanket and a hot cup of coffee while we relax on the swaying porch swing.

Long-time Fairhopers still refer to the "front" of a bay house as the side facing the bay. The back of the house faces the street. These "front porches" are usually quite large and may even hold tables and chairs to accommodate bay view brunches. Even a simple snack of tuna fish salad on a saltine and a glass of iced tea somehow tastes like royal fare when Mobile Bay is the view.

Many porches in town are traditionally appointed with beautiful outdoor furniture, swings, and of course, the traditional ferns. Yet you can also spot cast nets, fishing poles, or crab traps leaning to the side of the porch, awaiting the young fishermen arriving by the afternoon school bus.

Bright outdoor artwork of carved fishes or driftwood sculptures often decorates our porches with a personal Fairhope vibe, giving the visitor the message, "We're laid-back, casual, and love local art, so come on in."

Southerners have elevated the importance of the porch into a main room, although nowadays, home builders seem to have forgotten how much we appreciate this feature, just as they've abandoned the formal dining room where we love to gather, linger, and mingle over delicious food. Porches now seem to be an afterthought or caricature of the real thing. Not deep enough to hold a rocking chair that can actually be rocked, much less a swing or space for the cat to nap, porches on many newer homes are lacking in character, size, and charm.

One of my favorite touches on a porch can be found all over America, yet for some reason, is elevated to an art in Fairhope, and that's the addition of a porch lamp. Situated near the door or on a side table, the welcoming glow lets you know you're expected, wanted, and cared for. It says, "Let me make it easier for you to get inside." "Don't be afraid of the dark; here we are." The warmth elevates the porch into a beacon of friendliness.

A darling friend who lives alone in the neighborhood near the post office explained that even after the passing of her husband, she still has a glowing lamp on the porch every evening. "Even though I know he's not walking through the door, the lamp makes the house feel warm and I don't feel so alone. My home needs to be a place of beauty, even if I'm the only one here. I'm worth it, you know?" Yes, she is.

"Mabel" means "lovable," so that's the name we gave our first dog, whom we adopted from a shelter. It took her about four years to calm down and learn to relax on the front porch like a proper porch pooch. Before, we'd chase her around the neighborhood, waving a slice of ham, yelling, "Mabelene! Mabel! Come back here right now!"

The porch finally became a place of tranquility, with my husband often playing his guitar and Mabel keeping time with her tail. As I'd read to our boys, Mabel would listen. On fall afternoons, we'd watch leaves spin and, at night, tell ghost stories while the moon glowed and Mabel's ears twitched at the sound of nearby critters. At certain times of the year, the tree frogs were raucous to the point we literally couldn't carry on a conversation.

And every single night, no matter what we were doing, we'd cut on the lamp. Sitting atop a small table beside the kitchen screen door, it was the perfect glow of home. Familiar, like the spark in your lover's eyes.

Our porch days were illuminated by togetherness, music, little boys dressed in superhero costumes, storytelling, a dog who finally decided to stay put, and the warmth of a lamp.

To know we're worthy and loved enough to have someone leave the porch light on for us blesses our hearts. Even if we aren't expecting visitors, it somehow offers the finishing touch and completes the look, much like pearls on a pretty girl.

When Motel 6 adopted the genius slogan, "We'll leave the light on for you," they knew they'd hit a soft spot with Americans.

As we drive through Fairhope and pass house after house aglow with the golden light of a porch lamp, it's like a runway edged with directional lighting, pointing the way home. "This way to the people you love." "Straight ahead for a safe landing." And there, finally, is our own porch, aglow with the familiarity of home.

37

Why Thursdays?

While admiring his work on my dazzling Southern smile, dentist Douglas Harrell told me that businesses in downtown Fairhope were once closed every Thursday throughout the 1970s and many even into the 1980s. Vernon's Barber Shop is currently the one remaining business still observing the Thursday holiday. Dr. Harrell, who grew up in Fairhope, said he always wondered what was so special about Thursdays.

One possible reason for the midweek closure came from a social media post that speculated the trend began as a way to make time for the children to play ball games, in order to avoid playing on Sundays.

Dr. Harrell reasoned that maybe the sports connection was correct, but he also learned another interesting side of the story from the former postmaster, Robert Mason. It seems years ago, before the causeway was constructed in 1926, travel to and from Mobile was limited to the bay ferry, which offered half-price fares on, you guessed it — Thursday. Therefore, all the business owners in Fairhope closed up shop to sail to Mobile for supplies. The tradition remained when the more modern artery between Baldwin and Mobile counties was constructed. It was a practical way to insert an extra family day of rest, and perhaps youth baseball, into otherwise busy business owners' lives, and no one seemed to mind. Everyone enjoyed the extra free time so much that it gave them all big, dazzling Southern smiles, which Dr. Harrell's father, the late Dr. Harrell, was glad to care for in his dentist office, but not on Thursdays.

38

Campers in Love

"We built a fire on the beach, back far enough into the woods to make sure it was undetected." The man started the story as his wife gave a "here we go again" look and handed us cold drinks on the porch. He continued, "When the sunset turned the sky orange, we looked behind us to see if we could spot the moon rising from behind the pines, and sure enough, it was a bright, full moon." He went on, mimicking how the owls sounded, then slowed to take a deep breath and said with great seriousness, "We were officially out past dark." At this scandalous detail, he lowered his chin, raised his eyebrows, and added, "And you know what that means."

His wife laughed and called out from the kitchen, "Oh, cut that out!" She returned to the porch and filled in gaps in the story as the two of them recalled a lovely tale of a Fairhope romance.

Hot dogs stabbed with thin twigs roasted over the fire had somehow tasted better than any other meal they'd ever had. The runaways ate two dogs each and all the cookies they'd brought in a paper bag. The bottled Co-Colas were warm but washed everything down.

"What will we eat for breakfast?" Lisa asked.

"Remember the biscuits?" James reminded her.

"They'll be dry as dust by morning," she laughed.

Stars twinkled overhead while Mobile Bay's slow "slosh-slosh" lapped against the sand. Exhausted from a day of sailing, swimming, awkwardly dancing around "like fools," and running around being silly in the sand, the two 13-year-olds finally collapsed in laughter and took refuge in the old army tent James had taken from his parents' garage.

"They'll be looking for us by now," Lisa reasoned. She didn't care if her parents were angry because all she wanted to do was to be with James. He was the funniest best friend she'd ever had. They had known each other since the first grade but never paid much attention to one another until recently. He'd passed her a note during civics class at Fairhope Middle School three weeks earlier that said, "We'll get married someday."

When Lisa quietly slipped out of her house that afternoon, her father had been shaking the front page of the *Fairhope Courier* and mumbling something about President Johnson while her mother was organizing the refrigerator. "Meatloaf okay with everyone?" she called out to no one in particular.

It was hard to believe they'd been sitting in class just a day before. Eighth grade was unbearably dull, and they made plans to leave forever. Their teachers were uninformed, and the other students were childish. Today was the first part of their adventure that would last a lifetime.

In more modern times, both young teens would have been labeled as "gifted," but in 1966, they only had handwritten notes in their school files that said things like "overthinker" and "dreamer." The two described themselves as the only two rational people in town. "It's stifling to live in such a backward small place," James had said.

Meeting at the Fairhope Yacht Club, the two took a Sunfish and quickly made their way to an inlet south of the Grand Hotel. They never thought their summer sailing classes would be their ticket to freedom. Anchored in a spot where a house was boarded up for the season, they were sure no one would ever find them. Their supplies included a folded map of Tampa, books for reading on the long stretches of sailing open seas, a small purple transistor radio, a sketchbook, charcoal pencils, raw carrots, Nabs, four cold biscuits, and Cokes.

"Carrots are disgusting," he said.

She replied, "I love them, so get used to it."

James kicked sand on the fire and suggested they get some sleep. "I can't wait till we get to Key West," Lisa said. They didn't have a plan beyond their arrival in the Keys, but they read in the school library that it was tropical, and for the small-town Alabama teens, it held the symbol of freedom and big-world possibilities. In Florida, they'd finally escape their dreadful middle-school life.

With extreme fear, a shaky voice, and a smidgen of hope, James softly asked, "Do you love me?"

"I told you I do," insisted Lisa with a laugh and eye roll he couldn't see in the dark. Exhausted and feeling free yet still nervous to be so near and on the run, the two eighth graders fell into an exhausted sleep, boldly holding hands, with their hair smelling of bay water, hot dogs, and smoke.

Campers in Love

Frantic search parties of parents and friends combed the Eastern Shore, searching for the two children. The Fairhope police took to the airwaves of WABF to ask for the public's help locating the childhood friends.

The crashing end of the lovesick adventure boiled down to the tragic middle-school habit of oversleeping. The duo was exhausted and awoke midmorning to the barking of a dog and a man shaking their tent, yelling, "Hey! Hey! Are y'all the missing kids?" Their dream was destroyed when they separated after exiting the Fairhope police car. Lisa's father managed to keep the story out of the *Courier* the following week by appealing to the editor, Johnny Ferguson, who happened to be his fishing buddy, "They're just kids; give them a break." Most people in town forgot about the entire incident since everyone understands the pull of the bay on a moonlit night and the magic found in a friend turned into an innocent first love.

Lisa and James lost contact, not because of disinterest but because of embarrassment and parental control. Lisa's parents had enrolled her in a private school in Mobile, so there were few opportunities for contact. If she'd only known how much James still loved her, and if he'd only known how much Lisa still thought of their adventure, it would have all come together in a heartbeat, but in the days before social media, and at a time when boys and girls didn't just pick up the phone and call one another for fear of their parents answering, there may as well have been a million miles between them.

Once, amid a crowded downtown festival with artists, musicians, and juggling clowns, they had literally bumped into one another in front of the Fairhope Pharmacy. So shocked, their locked eyes grew wide, they couldn't speak, not for lack of words or thoughts, but because they didn't know where to begin. There was so much to say, yet just as he began to speak, James's friends had grabbed his arm and pulled him away while shouting something about a hamburger. So, completely dazed, he walked away, slumped over with heavy regret that followed him for years.

Time passed, and the two experienced separate colleges and the beginning of their first jobs until they finally reconnected as they overlooked the same bay where their adventure first began.

While packing up a Fourth of July picnic, Lisa looked into the night sky, still sizzling and popping with golden sparkles, and felt someone reach out and touch her arm. Before she even turned her head to look in his direction, she somehow knew it was him.

He stood in front of her, smiling, with the moonlight off Mobile Bay and the last of the fireworks reflecting in his eyes. After that night, they never left one another again.

This story was shared with me by very private people under the condition that I change the names of the campers for fear that their grandchildren would think they endorse 13-year-olds sneaking off together for camping adventures, but their story is true. Times have changed, and the innocence of childhood friends falling in love for a lifetime is almost unheard of, although passing notes at Fairhope Middle School is rumored to still be a popular activity. Hooting owls and splashing mullet can attest to the first sparks of love that continue until this very day in a house just south of the Grand Hotel, overlooking the bay, where a large family gathers to roast hot dogs over a fire, and a retired couple dances and laughs in the moonlight reflecting off Mobile Bay.

If you like ice cream, this is your town. I loved sitting on the huge roots of the oak tree on Church Street and eating Ye Olde Ice Cream as a child, and now love to drink Fairhope Floats from Mr. Gene's Beans. Living here with such kind people is a blessing and literally sweet!
— **Brett Jones**, Fairhope native and Realtor

39

Talent Beyond Limits

The sunsets may be all in his mind now, but they've never been more beautiful. Born in Fairhope in the old Jordan Clinic, where the Hampton Inn now sits, Ricky Trione enjoyed a typical Fairhope childhood and teen years, swimming and fishing in the bay and eating burgers at the A&W.

While still young, Ricky's artistic abilities emerged as he created remarkable pen and ink drawings of familiar hometown things like the Middle Bay Lighthouse and assorted wildlife.

Upon graduation from Fairhope High School, Ricky married his sweetheart Bonnie, whom he had met in middle school. She was the new girl with beautiful blonde hair. Enlisting in the U.S. Army, Ricky and

Bonnie lived as the All-American newlyweds. But life is never a perfect story, and Ricky, now a Captain, discovered this in a harsh way. While working on base, Ricky was involved in an unfortunate accident that sent a rock flying into his face, leaving him blind in his left eye. Bonnie cared for her husband and encouraged him to maintain normalcy, yet, in a story that seems too unfair and unreal, seven years later, while Ricky was stopped on the side of the road to check his car's engine, a passing truck blew a tire and the debris flew into Ricky's right eye. He was left completely blind.

Once again, Bonnie's love and encouragement, along with the care of his hometown friends, pulled him through a difficult time of transition.

Understandably frustrated and angry at first, Ricky's faith and natural ability to find joy helped him persevere. His good friend and art teacher, Vicky Nix Cook, explained to Ricky how he could adapt and continue to create his art even though things were dramatically different. Ricky remembered details of his childhood and recalled the beauty of his hometown. Although he couldn't see outward things, Ricky still had the inward eye of an artist and beautiful memories.

"Vicky is a wonderful artist and teacher and began showing me how to create art using texture as a guide," Ricky said. Navigating his way around a paint palette by memorizing a color sequence and finding his way around town became new challenges.

Even old friends initially found it awkward when they first encountered their old friend who was newly blind. Once, while Ricky stood on the corner of Section Street and Fairhope Avenue, a man approached and said, "Would you like some help crossing the street?"

"Sure," replied Ricky, glad for the kind offer.

But before he could give directions on extending his arm for guidance, the relatively large man gave Ricky a full bear hug, lifted him off his feet, and carried him to the other side, plopping him down beneath the town clock. "I didn't know what to say," Ricky laughed.

The memory of the bear-hug street crossing was still fresh on his mind when Page and Palette bookstore asked Ricky to participate in their "Safety Day." Paramedics, firefighters, and police officers, along with their emergency vehicles, were on hand to discuss important safety issues with children. Ricky was invited to speak on how to offer assistance to the visually impaired.

The children loved Ricky. "Can I help you cross the street?" one child asked. "Sure," Ricky replied. The children gathered outside on the flower-filled corner and watched with great interest as Ricky unfolded his white cane and tapped it on the ground a few times. The child proudly escorted Mr. Ricky across the street. Everyone cheered when he arrived safely on the opposite corner.

Then another child called out, "I'll help you back over to this side!" Once again, the path was retraced to great shouts of celebration. Then another child cried out, "But I want a turn to help Mr. Ricky!" Being a good sport, Ricky walked across the street, holding the shoulder of the child while everyone watched his every step. The children who guided him puffed up and felt very important in their role as a real community helper and guide of this fine man.

"I ended up crossing that street about 30 times that day," Ricky laughed. His sense of humor and good nature couldn't let him say no to any child.

Ricky continues in his passion for art, surprising many with his ability to use textured paints and his vivid memory of days spent playing on Mobile Bay. He visits schools to demonstrate that even though his ability to create art is different than before, it hasn't been taken away. Inspiring children to find their talent beyond limits is what keeps Ricky motivated.

Sitting on a bench overlooking Mobile Bay, Bonnie describes the sunsets to Ricky and says, "The sun is deep orange with pink clouds on either side. It's two fingers above the horizon."

"Living in my hometown with all of my friends has been healing and a source of joy" Ricky said.

"The sun's now one finger above the horizon."

"Fairhope is just as beautiful to me today as it was when I was a little boy fishing with my dad."

"And now the sun has disappeared, and the sky is a mixture of pink and deep blue."

"I can't wait to paint it tomorrow."

The Eastern Shore Art Center sponsored a city-wide "Art on a Limb" yarn bombing in 2016 to decorate downtown trees, light posts, and buildings.

40

928 Is Oh, So Great

It wasn't all that long ago that if you were running for local political office and your phone number didn't begin with the "928" prefix, you were doomed. To this day, older businesses, churches, and other landline establishments still proudly maintain their 928 status symbol.

When I moved to town, the "new folks" were just starting to be assigned a dreaded "990" number, but for some reason, our household was bestowed the blessed prize of the coveted old 928. After I gave my number to a new acquaintance, she almost spilled her lime sherbet punch and gasped, "How did YOU get a 928 number?" I wasn't offended, just amused at her method of welcoming me to town.

Even though cell phones have scrambled us together in numerical chaos, my clever husband figured out how to preserve the home's landline 928 number for my cellular use. That man is pure gold at times. I uphold the 928 tradition, while the shocked woman now probably has a cell phone with some strange numerical combination I can only hope is the code for Detroit.

If someone looks confused when I give them my cell phone number, and they pause to ask, "Is that really your cell?" I know they recognize the 928 and have deep Fairhope roots. It's a lingering connection to the old ways of the past, in a new-fangled technological sort of way.

41

Meanwhile At the Clubhouse

"I don't know what this club would do without me," thought Mattie Mae. "I'm the only one around here who can make good coffee." She finished filling the big pot with water then busied herself with folding the napkins into perfectly pointed triangles.

It was her self-imposed duty to arrive early and set everything up since she knew she was the most excellent hostess east of the Mississippi. Other members pitched in to help with the name tag table, refreshments, and the very important table decorations, which set the tone for the meeting.

Southerners have a knack for turning just about anything into a good club. Whether it's a book, game, flower, dinner, animal, or even salvation, we can find a cause for meeting. The menfolk match us club-for-club with their own groups for hunting, stamps, go-karts, sports, little choo-choo trains, cars, and of course, charities, to keep them humble.

The October of 2018 meeting of the Fairhope Yacht Club Ladies' Auxiliary was one of chaos after Deenie volunteered to provide the autumnal table centerpieces. Her sailboat sculptures made from pinecones, acorns, and moss-covered twigs were, at first glance, adorable. She even used big orange fall leaves for the boat's sails, which had to be pressed between pages of a book and shipped to her from her sister's home in Virginia, since Fairhope has no colorful fall leaves. But poor Deenie didn't realize that before you can use Southern pinecones, twigs, and acorns indoors, you must first bake them in a warm oven or zap them in the microwave to kill the creepy-crawly critters that lurk inside.

A few minutes after the meeting was called to order, "with liberty and justice for all" was mixed with gasps, screams, and spewing of words only sailor ladies know as they watched the naturally nautical boats come to life with crawling mites, ants, spiders, and some sort of tick.

Shirley used the president's gavel to smash bugs like Whac-a-Mole while Darleen dumped her iced tea on the arrangement and Carolyn, with a worm of some sort dangling from her wrist, flung the door open, as one by one the all-natural table centerpieces were flung into the harbor.

The club members declared it to be the best meeting of the year and nursed their ant bites with lunches of chicken salad and extra midday champagne.

Meanwhile At the Clubhouse

With approximately 12 garden clubs in Fairhope, it's no wonder we're abloom year-round and, at times, smell like a carnation-filled funeral home. There's a garden club for those who actually get their hands dirty and keep a bucket in the trunk of their car with a small shovel and clippers, just in case they pass your house and see something that needs "sharing." Their unofficial motto is, "Don't shoot, I'm from the garden club!"

Another garden club dedicates their time to planning designs for their subdivision entryway, while another, named "Soiled Rotten," focuses on discussing the stunning floral arrangements sent by their husbands each month.

Not into gardening at all, The Mimosa Garden Club only sips them. The newest garden club in town only meets to review books about gardens while wearing floral prints. See? There's something for everyone.

Sewing clubs, ukulele clubs, bird-watching clubs, doll clubs, and — I kid you not — a mulching club, where members are encouraged to bring their food scraps, are all real things around here.

Marybeth was overjoyed to snag a placement on the coveted Committee for the Preservation of Loveliness, Baby-Naming Subcommittee, which always awards an engraved silver tray to the best-named infant in town. It's a grand honor to have your precious babe acknowledged at a wedge salad luncheon held each spring in a private home. Last year, the honor went to little Charlotte Azalea Clower. Little "Lottie," taken from "Charlotte," was officially Fairhope's best-named baby.

"An excellent nod to our floral heritage," said Luveena. "Brilliant monogram and nickname potential," bubbled Liza Jo.

"Mmm. Is that coffee I smell?" called out Marybeth.

"It sure is, honey; come on in and get some while it's fresh," Mattie Mae told her.

Marybeth said, "Hold on, I can't walk very fast. I'm wearing my sitting shoes today."

Mattie Mae dried her hands on a tea towel that said "Fairhope" with a little heart in place of the "o," sighed deeply, and whispered, "I just love meeting days."

42

Good, Bad, and Ugly

While I was dragging my toes through the sand, a pelican soared close enough to my head to create a breeze and shouted, "If you want to live amongst the roses, beware of the thorns!" Pelicans are a bit frightening, but they're pretty smart.

By illuminating Fairhope's kindness, I may have erroneously led you to believe our jails are empty. Quite the contrary, but true to form, even our villains are creative in their sins.

Until recently, the Fairhope Police Department only dealt with childhood pranks gone too far, like rearranging the neighbor's front lawn Christmas reindeer into lewd positions, Mardi Gras overindulgence, and the occasional disputed property line issues. Still, within the last decade, they've seen far more severe problems, reflecting the larger world in which we live. It's a dark place out there, and the shadows of evil are falling on small towns like Fairhope.

Even with these advancements in serious crimes, our uniqueness extends to the dastardly crooks. Chopping down trees on public property to make a grown-up tree fort is one of the best uses of a misdemeanor I've ever heard of, and our officers have plenty of unique calls dealing with situations like the ostrich that was dodging in and out of traffic. "It turned out to be an emu," said the calm, knowledgeable officer who responded to the call. The simple message on the city's social media site said, "If you're missing your emu, give us a call." "Only in Fairhope," everyone commented. We've also spotted wayward donkeys, cows, and camels, usually around the time Trinity Presbyterian presents its live Christmas nativity scene.

A rash of car burglaries took place in the mid-1990s when a band of robbers from another county went driveway to driveway, searching for loot in unlocked cars. They were finally apprehended red-handed, holding bags containing iconic Fairhope treasures, such as expensive sunglasses, Disney movies, carwash passes, four handguns, assorted tools, and two Bibles. Four of those things got them in big trouble.

Good, Bad, and Ugly

Sadly, drugs, domestic abuse, theft, and other terrible crimes keep our police force busy these days. It's nothing new to the world, yet it still rattles us when we hear about troubling situations in our small community.

While being pulled in a wagon behind a Clydesdale on the rocky island of Inisheer, I met a man from a large city in California, and together, we wondered if there was a crime problem on an island with only 300 lads and lassies. He said it didn't matter which side of the law you were on in his hometown; everyone feared and disliked the police.

"We take cookies to our police," I told him. He almost fell off the wagon. I continued, "They decorate the police station for Halloween and give the children candy. The police officers also provide backpacks filled with school supplies to children in need." He questioned whether I'd tipped a few Irish pints.

Offering citizen police academies to the public builds bridges of communication and trust throughout the community. The Fairhope police are always available to visit and speak at community and school events, keeping their presence visible to all who rely on their help.

Yes, things are pretty rosy around here, but heed the advice of the pelican and beware the thorns, for they can truly hurt.

Over 200,000 people attend the annual Fairhope Arts and Crafts Festival each Spring.

43

The Surprise at the Museum

The large old-timey safe that looked like it came from a John Wayne western, sat in the corner of the old city hall. When the decision was made to convert the 1928 Spanish Mission-style building into a museum, the safe needed to be cracked open and cleared. What could be inside? No one could remember. Gold bars? A treasure map? A long-lost last will and testament? Where do you find a stethoscope-wearing safe-cracker these days?

Not that I'm partial, but I think the Fairhope Museum of History is one of the best small-town museums I've ever seen. Featuring both rotating exhibits and a permanent collection, it tells the story of our town in a way you won't forget. With free admission and cool air-conditioning, it's the perfect first stop for out-of-town visitors.

The building was originally used as the Fairhope City Hall and later served as the police station. When I moved here, it was empty and used only during Halloween when the Fairhope Police Department turned it into a haunted house. Local children would stand in line to enter the spooky building, where goblins would pop out and a scary dude would chase the children with a chainsaw – the non-cutting type, I'm sure, but it evoked screams of fright from the crowd.

The town's creative minds went wild with ideas of what the locked safe could hold. Rumors swirled, and on the day of the "grand opening," a crowd gathered, including newspaper and TV reporters. I took my sons to watch the drama since it was the perfect entertainment for little boys, and when the TV reporter asked one of them what he thought was inside, he said, "A sandwich."

After a few whirls, taps, and spins of the dial, the heavy door creaked open. Everyone held their breath, and the city officials handling the event peered inside the dark safe, only to find "contraband" with a resident's name attached. The evidence in this case had been forgotten, and they made the quick, gentlemanly decision that the long-ago guilty deserved a second chance, so the door was quickly closed without anyone naming names. The mystery was immediately declared to be "nothing, positively nothing," and the officials closed the door so quickly that I've always suspected it was one of their names. Surely not.

The Surprise at the Museum

Donnie Barrett headed up the inception and much of the design of the museum, serving as the first director as well as the heart and soul of each exhibit. Donnie's wealth of knowledge was second only to his passion for Fairhope, and the public loved his dry wit and sense of humor when it came to sharing little-known and amazing facts about the city he loves. Donnie brought enthusiasm and charm to the city by organizing the Elderberry Festival, Round-Up Day, and plays in the cemetery where costumed actors portrayed the city founders standing near their actual graves.

One afternoon, Donnie allowed my sons to use their new GoPro camera to make a movie about someone who was escaping from jail. The old jail cell, still inside the museum, with heavy iron bars, was the perfect backdrop for their first attempt at cinematic greatness. All these years later, my sons are employed in the videography and film industry, and to think, it all started at the museum.

I've always loved the story Donnie told about another teen in town who entered the cell. His mischievous friends clicked the door shut behind him, took the big iron key, and left. The poor kid was locked inside, and when he shouted for help, Donnie said he couldn't do anything without the key. He knew where it was all along, but in a panic, the boy used his cell phone to call his mother, telling her how he ended up locked in the old jail. "Do something!" he insisted. I don't know who she was, but surely we'd be friends because when she showed up to "save" her son, she only handed him bread and water through the bars, fake cried, and said, "Where did I go wrong?"

Donnie has since retired, but others continue to fill his role as museum director and keeper of Fairhope history. And the safe is still in the museum for all to see, securely locked, with absolutely nothing, positively nothing inside — nothing, whatsoever.

44

Twilight Wish

Of course, it's your decision
To grow cotton or new house sites
But for now, you've kept the cows
It's the wish I wish tonight

The scorched pumpkin sky deepens
With a descending red balloon
Silhouetted calves leap and stretch —
The cow jumped over the moon

Leslie Anne Tarabella

A bright pearl of white shines high
In the glowing November sky
Thinking fast, I make a wish
As the little bulls strut by

Next time I pass by this field
The snorting bulls may be replaced
By loud bulldozers pushing
Building progress with great haste

The first star claims my wishes
Field and farms to remain the same
Pillowed cotton, rows of corn
And little bulls playing games

It's your wide field of choices
How to manage the old and new
But tonight while traveling home
My first twilight wish came true

45

Could We Be Paris?

All grand cities began small.

Do you think hundreds of years ago, François and Pierre were leaning against a fence, sipping un café in old "Par-ee" while lamenting the construction of Notre Dame?

"Ahh . . . what a monstrosity," said François.

"Oui, oui," said Pierre as he nibbled his croissant, "Everything is changing so fast!"

They continued voicing their dissatisfaction. "Yes, I can barely recognize Paris anymore. The influx of the neoteric crowd, destroying perfectly good cottages and constructing atrocities that tower over the Seine."

Fairhope is no Paris, but Paris had to begin somewhere. It once had rolling pastures with enough cows and goats to provide stinky cheese for all of France. By the time they constructed the Eiffel Tower, the public had complained about the change, and some said the tower would be an eyesore. French author Henri René Albert Guy de Maupassant (try monogramming that on a towel) referred to the tower as "this high and skinny pyramid of iron ladders, this giant ungainly skeleton."

The ornate opera house, Palais Garnier, was undoubtedly a shock to those who had been living in the outlying countryside. "What's wrong with Fifi's Pub? There's a piano and room for an accordion player. We don't need no dang opera house!" "Yeah, that's for fancy new people coming in and changing everything! Next thing you know, they'll want bistros to open on Mondays and serve champagne on the Lord's Day!"

We all know the story ended with the world falling in love with the City of Lights. People flock to Paris for its fabulous food, to see the Eiffel Tower, and to experience its famous "Je ne sais quoi."

Can we really imagine ourselves as a smaller version of Paris, New York, or Rome right here on the Gulf Coast? Don't laugh so hard. It took

Could We Be Paris?

centuries for these cities to develop into iconic locations, so if we could see Fairhope 100 or 300 years into the future, would it be or could it be as grand? Could it be as iconic in a smaller way?

We could substitute NASCAR for Le Mans and oysters on the half-shell for escargot. Notre Dame would become Baptist with dinner on the grounds rivaling Le Cordon Bleu. It sounds delightfully Southern and totally plausible in a Rip Van Winkle sort of dream.

The former president of Samford University, Dr. Andrew Westmoreland, was fond of the quote, "We sit in the shade of trees others have planted." What are we planting for our future? City councils and activists debate and explore options for bicycle lanes, building height restrictions, and our unique Single Tax Corporation. The decisions we make now will determine what others experience in the future.

Perhaps our angst shouldn't focus on the number of residents pouring into town but instead examine our own version of "je ne sais quoi," or "I don't know what — I can't exactly put my finger on what it is."

The heartbeat of a city should remain constant even when its outward body changes shape. Buildings come and go, as do people, but maintaining the unique personality of a place should be our goal. In 200 years, will Fairhope still be a city of enchantment? Will we still be known for our

Southern charm and hospitality tinged with great thinkers, dreamers, and sailors, or will we slowly swirl down the drain into a great pool of blandness?

Other beautiful cities and heritage sites have banned or highly restricted unimaginative chain stores. They've demanded chains meet their characteristic standards. The McDonald's in Freeport, Maine, is located inside an old Greek-Revival style home that was going to be destroyed until the public lobbied for using it for another purpose. Other American cities have required drug stores, fast food, and grocery chains to meet their local regulations to maintain the city's character. Fairhope leaders should consider requiring the same. You can be small and still flex your muscles.

What would small town guidelines look like for Fairhope? We have so many different forms of architecture it would be hard to name a specific style, but "coastal-Southern-floral-rural-chic" is a start. Easy, right? And don't forget the Spanish Mission influence as well.

Then again, we also live in a place where people don't like others telling them what to do — oh dear, let the hand-wringing begin.

Are we Paris? Some would laugh at the thought. But then again, François and Pierre returned to their farms, thinking it was just a bunch of wild dreamers bringing crazy ideas into their small village. They chuckled, "Paris a major city?" "Très drôle, it will never happen."

46

Dear Florala

I was shocked that I wasn't shocked. Does that make sense?

When I read that Baldwin County is now the seventh fastest-growing metro area in the country, according to the U.S. Census Bureau, I wasn't surprised, yet I still had to let it sink in. We're seventh in growth in the entire United States of America. We're hanging out in the mix with Austin, Texas, and Orlando, Florida. This made me feel all swimmy-headed, as my Walton County, Florida, grandmother would say.

Like the aftershocks of a bomb, rapid growth is rippling in waves across our entire area. I knew Navarre, Florida, when it was only known for its bridge that cost a quarter to cross and a few small hotels, and now it's got all the big-city traffic and accessories it can hold. Destin started the trend in the early 1980s when locals looked out their windows one morning and saw developers scrambling over the pristine sand dunes like a kicked-over bed of fire ants.

And speaking of my grandmother, South Walton County's legal issues are tangling up faster than a kid's fishing line. New waterfront homeowners have interpreted property laws to mean they own every grain of sand up to the edge of the Gulf of Mexico. The local folks who grew up playing on those beaches, like my grandmother and a long line of relatives before and after her, now have no access to the water.

A Chicago couple recently paid a record 8.5 million dollars for a home in the perfect spot to watch dolphins and hurricanes. When people spend that much money, you can see how they don't want to cut their heels on the pop tops of local riff-raff who hang out on their patch of sand. It's yet another mess of growth no one could have predicted. Everyone is frustrated except for the realtors, developers, and lawyers.

To our west, the Mississippi coastline isn't immune to growth, with Gulfport being one of the fastest-growing cities in the Magnolia State. But will there be ripples of growth inland as well? Lovely Florala, home of the largest natural lake in Alabama, and nearby Monroeville saw declining populations in past decades when major roads were rerouted, and factories closed. Will they be rediscovered and catch the overflow from their nearby

Dear Florala

coastal neighbors? I feel like slipping them a note that says, "Dear Florala, be careful what you wish for. Love, Fairhope."

The Duck Pond at the Fairhope Municipal Pier and Park is a popular spot for walkers and joggers.

47

Just Because You Can Doesn't Mean You Should

What was once a tiny town of considerable characters is now six times its size and populated by appalling people.
— **Harper Lee,** describing her hometown of Monroeville, Alabama, in a letter to her friend Charles Carruth

A developer in Dallas, Texas, plans to construct 600 new homes in a rural area of Fairhope. The infrastructure can't accommodate higher traffic, so new roads will have to be built. Schools will be overloaded, so the funds must be found to expand schools and hire new teachers.

Developers get a bad name in situations like this, but it's legal. It's the American way. It's supply and demand, but does that make it right?

Two quaint homes on a shady downtown street are surrounded by other homes that have been there since the mid-1900s. A local resident purchased the houses and plans to replace them with a commercial building. It will lower the value of the surrounding homes since they will face commercial property, and parking will now be an issue. On that stretch of street, lined with large overhanging oaks, it's legal, but just because you can do it, is it right? This developer isn't from out of town. He's a Fairhope citizen, so can we be angry with our friend? He's following the law.

What if a church or business wants to demolish nearby houses for their occasional parking needs, causing a drop in the value of surrounding homes? Who is to blame them if they bought the property fair and square?

Older cities have learned that spreading apartments throughout the city in small numbers is far more desirable than clumping 500 of them together. Still, at this time, local zoning is allowing massive complexes to be constructed, sure to bring more problems down the newly widened road.

Discussions are heated, and everyone has their own interpretation of laws and civic morality. Efforts to control growth and protect the neighborhoods have failed due to the independent nature of people, who

Just Because You Can Doesn't Mean You Should

don't want anyone to tell them what they can and can't do with their own property.

We can all understand both sides of this contentious issue.

Some people say that replacing an eyesore house with a better house is okay, but who's to decide what is "better"? Others want everything to remain unchanged, even if it's falling apart.

One home builder actually said the neighbor should thank him for building a towering house that blocks the sunlight on the smaller next-door cottage. "His utility bill will be lower now." More than once, someone has said, "I hate all these new houses in my neighborhood," but thanks to the new houses on the street, they were able to sell their 1965 ranch-style home for $800,000 more than they'd originally paid.

This story will eventually apply to every other small town along the Gulf Coast and beyond. Even the larger cities of Mobile and Pensacola are seeing shifts with some neighborhoods booming while others struggle.

It's all a big mess.

Historic properties aren't protected, and residents have repeatedly voted down efforts for zoning regulations yet complain loudly on social media if a change occurs. The tide may finally be turning with new calls for preservation, but it's a slow process and many projects are already "on the books," so they'll be allowed.

It's yet another reason everyone is on edge at best and furious with their neighbor at worst. With developers hiding behind corporation names, anger is often misplaced on those buying the homes and renting the offices, while the developers count their money back in Texas. Or down the street in Fairhope.

48

Before You Call the Moving Truck

These stories about my hometown may have found you in a place far removed from Fairhope. You may be reading about our town feeling relieved you don't live in such a hokey-goofy-sappy-hot as the Devil's furnace kind of place. You're thinking how threatened you'd feel if people descended upon you as you were moving into your new house and asked you millions of questions about where you were from and who your people were.

Then again, maybe you're jealous.

You may long for petunias atop your downtown garbage cans and a good family-friendly parade. You call your city council members and ask, "Why can't our downtown have a pajama-movie night in the streets?"

But wait; differences are to be celebrated, and community spirit can be found wherever you live. Our uniqueness has served us well, but other cities have their own wonderful personalities.

Corporate America has tried to make the entire country look the same by plopping identical stores selling identical wares on identical strips of highways. It's easier for them to market to one type of town than those with specific preferences. Multimedia options have blurred regional accents and given us the same opinions, jokes, and news as everyone else. Musical styles have fused, and the internet makes it possible to hear live Southern gospel or New Orleans jazz from anywhere in the world.

Down-home Southern restaurants that serve grits and collard greens in New York City bother me, just as a bowl of clam chowder in Pigeon Forge, Tennessee, seems wrong.

Our country is fascinating because of our regional differences, which should be preserved and celebrated.

Before You Call the Moving Truck

So, before you pack your car and contact a realtor in Fairhope, why don't you look at your own city's beauty and spirit? You may have picked up on the secret to our success in these stories.

We often see out-of-town delegations taking pictures of our flower beds and measuring the sidewalks in the hopes of taking some of that charm back home. But let me save you some time. The secret to Fairhope's charm can't be measured.

Our secret is that the people are connected.

It's not the flowers, bay, parades, or cute dogs that make this a desirable place to live. It's because we join together with others to get things done. Even if the "getting done" only includes watching a movie, we see it's done right with a lecture series and film festival, or at least with good friends. We join with others to feed the hungry, clothe the needy, build a house, support our police, read to children, and save the animals. We clean dirty water and write poetry. We identify birds and write song lyrics. We join together to protest big-store sprawl, and we gather in prayer on the bluff. We join one another for absolutely everything. This means our groups of friends intersect, so we know each other well.

If Fairhope were a math equation, we'd be a giant Venn diagram representing relationships between people, with the intersecting circles overlapping one another, time after time, reflecting our abundance of commonalities, even when we're very different.

Susie belongs to the Ukulele Club, where she gets to know Chip, who also teaches a woodworking class through the Eastern Shore Art Center. George signs up for his class so he can make a clock, then meets Susie while they are working at Ecumenical Ministries thrift shop, and they suddenly realize they both know Chip. They realize how much they have in common, even though they belong to different churches and vote for different candidates. This kind of thing happens all the time.

We're connected through joining. Participation in life is essential, no matter where you live. If you can get people to participate and connect, beautiful things will follow.

If you removed Fairhope's community groups, civic clubs, churches, book clubs, band boosters and pickleball teams, all that would remain is steaming hot summers, mosquitoes, and dusty peanut fields. We're nothing special without connections.

Other places can't make themselves become Fairhope, yet they can find their own unique identity when the people begin to connect.

Before You Call the Moving Truck

All it takes is one person with enthusiasm. When invited, others will join, and connections will blossom. Then you will begin to see all that is beautiful within your own hometown.

But you're welcome to come measure our flower beds if you insist.

Mobile Bay is the perfect spot for a sunset picnic.

49

Worthy of Praise

Around 1500, early Spanish explorers created rustic maps and labeled Mobile Bay as "Bahía del Espíritu Santo" or "Bay of the Holy Spirit."

If you've ever stared out onto the waters of Mobile Bay, you've felt it. The feeling of holiness is there for believers who recognize it, while even non-believers understand there's something different about this place.

If there is one Bible verse that reminds me of Fairhope, it is this:

"Finally, brethren, whatever things are true, whatever things are noble, whatever things are just, whatever things are pure, whatever things are lovely, whatever things are of good report, if there is any virtue and if there is anything praiseworthy — meditate on these things." (Philippians 4:8, English Standard Version)

When couples walk hand in hand along the pier or children's laughter can be heard from Fairhoper's Park, this is indeed a pure and lovely place.

When widows gather to play cards at the Nix Center, and new friendships are formed late in life, this is indeed a commendable, excellent place.

When I lift my hand to shield my eyes from the mirror-like glare of the water, it's a hometown salute that acknowledges God's stunning creation as indeed worthy of praise.

The Spanish explorers got it right the first time, and many of us still feel the Bahía del Espíritu Santo today.

50

Goodbye to Fairhope

"Hello" is more precious when we remember it will always be followed by "goodbye."

If you're leaving us after a refreshing weekend visit, moving on to retirement, leaving to be near family, or maybe even taking off to follow love — it was nice having you here, and we're sorry to say farewell.

Goodbyes apply to people, places, eras, trends, and all the days in between. Fairhope has already said goodbye to most of our dirt roads, a wooden city pier, a large bayfront hotel, and too many fine boats to count. And yet, we still welcome the new.

Begrudgingly, open-armed, or skeptically, we've become good at welcoming, time after time. It's now a necessary way of life.

Whatever incarnation of Fairhope is left to future generations, be it wooded bluffs overlooking sparkling water, small fishing shacks, cornfields, mansions, skyscrapers, or spaceships, there will always be room for another true Fairhoper.

One hundred years from now, the local folks will still say there's too much growth, and newcomers will repeat, "If we'd only arrived ten years earlier."

Will futuristic Fairhopers find continued beauty and a thriving city, or will today's missteps lead to destruction and decay?

The city founders were wise to reserve waterfront property for public use, but what will we leave for the enjoyment of those yet to come? Will they think our generation was as creative and bold as the founders, or do we allow the naysayers on social media who label progress as "monstrosities," "outlandish," and "risky" to dictate our every decision?"

It's sad when things change, yet it's also sad when they don't.

The future we welcome will be different yet familiar. Season after season, sailors will return from the salty bay to an ever-changing harbor. The bulbs beneath the ground will bloom in flower beds for new faces that don't remember us. Small acorns we kick down the street today will shade future picnics, and our beautiful new homes, which now stand on sites once occupied by small wooden houses, will someday be called "outdated" and replaced by a futuristic definition of beauty and function.

But as long as there's the hope of home in someone's heart and people want a place to belong, a place to create and a place to love, there will be someone who will slip through the hedge and find their way to Fairhope, Alabama.

There's no need to push.

Acknowledgments

I agree with you; there are fifty other stories about Fairhope I should have included. There's no way to tell all the amazing things about a small town because, day by day, new stories emerge and, with time, become legends. Thanking everyone who inspired and reviewed these stories is challenging for fear of inadvertently omitting someone, but of course, the easy place to begin is with my wildly talented family. Bob, Joseph, and Harrison spark my creativity and offer excellent feedback. I wouldn't have such wonderful material without the experiences of our hometown champions, Pete Blohme, Leslie Presson, Ricky and Bonnie Trione, Louis and Melinda Mapp, and Lori Terral, who graciously shared their stories with me. A significant boost of enthusiasm came from the colorful and knowledgeable Donnie Barrett, along with Santa's main guy and friend,

Cecil Christenberry. I'm also indebted to friends who shared their love of Fairhope: Ann Miller, Mike Lyons, Harriet Outlaw, Brett Jones, Barbara Wheeler, Dee Washington, Tamara Wintzell, William Stitt, Jule Moon, J.D. Crowe, Dr. Douglas Harrell, Malia Mullican, Sharon Davis, Leslie West, John Sharp, and the amazing Andy Andrews, who inspires me and loves his corner of Baldwin County as much as I love mine. I'd also like to thank my early readers and friends, Rachel Bowen Frey, Ron Meszaros, Alan Samry, and editor Jasmine Hodges. A big Cảm ơn (thank you) to Khanh Mai for his translation assistance. I certainly can't forget to thank The City of Fairhope employees and current and past elected officials who are dedicated to preserving our hometown traditions and spirit of creative adventure.

I also give a heartfelt thanks to you, my supportive readers, and invite you to follow me at leslieannetarabella.com.

About the Author

As a South Alabama native who has spent most of her life along the Gulf Coast, Leslie Anne Tarabella has lived in Fairhope, Alabama, since 1999, where she and her husband raised their two sons. Leslie Anne won a humor award for her weekly newspaper column, *Southern with a Gulf Coast Accent*, which she wrote for ten years. With a knack for local culture, Leslie Anne was the natural choice to author an encompassing tourism guide for Orange Beach and Gulf Shores, Alabama. She also co-authored a guidebook for Downtown Fairhope. Her books include *The Majorettes are Back in Town*, and *Exploding Hushpuppies*, which are collections of her reader's favorite columns. Her true story for all ages, *Bringing Christmas Home*, was named the Barnes and Noble Holiday Book of the Year.

www.ingramcontent.com/pod-product-compliance
Lightning Source LLC
Chambersburg PA
CBHW020334010526
44119CB00002B/59